The Future of Work Series

Series Editor: **Peter Nolan**, Director of the ESRC Future of Work Programme and the Montague Burton Professor of Industrial Relations at Leeds University Business School in the UK.

Few subjects could be judged more vital to current policy and academic debates than the prospects for work and employment. *The Future of Work* series provides the much needed evidence and theoretical advances to enhance our understanding of the critical developments most likely to impact on people's working lives.

Titles include:

Chris Baldry, Peter Bain, Phil Taylor, Jeff Hyman, Dora Scholarios, Abigail Marks, Aileen Watson, Kay Gilbert, Gregor Gall and Dirk Bunzel
THE MEANING OF WORK IN THE NEW ECONOMY

Harriet Bradley and Geraldine Healy
ETHNICITY AND GENDER AT WORK
Identity, Careers and Employment Relations

Julia Brannen, Peter Moss and Ann Mooney
WORKING AND CARING OVER THE TWENTIETH CENTURY
Change and Continuity in Four Generation Families

Andy Danford, Mike Richardson, Paul Stewart, Stephanie Tailby and Martin Upchurch
PARTNERSHIP AND THE HIGH PERFORMANCE WORKPLACE
Work and Employment Relations in the Aerospace Industry

Geraldine Healy, Edmund Heery, Phil Taylor and William Brown (*editors*)
THE FUTURE OF WORKER REPRESENTATION

Diane Houston (*editor*)
WORK-LIFE BALANCE IN THE 21st CENTURY

Theo Nichols and Surhan Cam
LABOUR IN A GLOBAL WORLD
Case Studies from the White Goods Industry in Africa, South America, East Asia and Europe

Paul Stewart (*editor*)
EMPLOYMENT, TRADE UNION RENEWAL AND THE FUTURE OF WORK
The Experience of Work and Organisational Change

Clare Ungerson and Sue Yeandle (*editors*)
CASH FOR CARE IN DEVELOPED WELFARE STATES

Martin Upchurch, Andy Danford, Stephanie Tailby and Mike Richardson
THE REALITIES OF PARTNERSHIP AT WORK

Michael White, Stephen Hill, Colin Mills and Deborah Smeaton
MANAGING TO CHANGE?
British Workplaces and the Future of Work

The Future of Work Series

Series Standing Order ISBN 978-1-4039-1477-4

You can receive future titles in this series as they are published by placing a standing order. Please contact your bookseller or, in case of difficulty, write to us at the address below with your name and address, the title of the series and one of the ISBNs quoted above.

Customer Services Department, Macmillan Distribution Ltd, Houndmills, Basingstoke, Hampshire RG21 6XS, England

The Realities of Partnership at Work

Martin Upchurch

Andy Danford

Stephanie Tailby

Mike Richardson

First published 2008 by
PALGRAVE MACMILLAN

Palgrave Macmillan in the UK is an imprint of Macmillan Publishers Limited, registered in England, company number 785998, of Houndmills, Basingstoke, Hampshire RG21 6XS.

Palgrave Macmillan in the US is a division of St Martin's Press LLC, 175 Fifth Avenue, New York, NY 10010.

Palgrave Macmillan is the global academic imprint of the above companies and has companies and representatives throughout the world.

Palgrave® and Macmillan® are registered trademarks in the United States, the United Kingdom, Europe and other countries.

ISBN-13: 978-0-230-00697-3   hardback
ISBN-10: 0-230-00697-3   hardback

This book is printed on paper suitable for recycling and made from fully managed and sustained forest sources. Logging, pulping and manufacturing processes are expected to conform to the environmental regulations of the country of origin.

A catalogue record for this book is available from the British Library.

Library of Congress Cataloging-in-Publication Data

The realities of partnership at work / Martin Upchurch ... [et al.].
    p. cm.
Includes bibliographical references and index.
ISBN-13: 978-0-230-00697-3 (alk. paper)
1. Industrial relations—Great Britain.   2. Labor unions—Great Britain.
3. Management—Employee participation—Great Britain.
I. Upchurch, Martin, 1951–

HD8391.R43 2008
331.8801—dc22   2008020658

10 9 8 7 6 5 4 3 2 1
17 16 15 14 13 12 11 10 09 08

Printed and bound in Great Britain by
CPI Antony Rowe, Chippenham and Eastbourne

Contents

List of Figures   vii

List of Tables   viii

Notes on the Authors   x

Acknowledgements   xi

1 Partnership at Work   **1**
What is partnership?   1
A new productive base?   5
The TUC and partnership   7
Partnership as a 'Third Way' project   10
Critics from within and without   14
The studies   18

2 The High-Performance Workplace: Fact or Fiction?   **20**
High-performance work practices and worker attributes   23
Work intensity and job recomposition   27
Task discretion   30
Job satisfaction   34
Employee commitment   37
Staff consultation   41
Workplace stress   44
Union performance   47
Conclusion   51

3 Gambling with Employee Voice in the Finance Sector   **53**
The finance sector   53
Employee relations strategies   62
Employees' attitudes to voice and representation   69
Conclusion: Gambling with the paradox of intention   81

4 Best Value in a Local Authority   **84**
The role of local trade unions   87
Security of employment, the intensification of work and   92
job satisfaction

Employee involvement   100
Conclusion   103

5 **Partnership on Prescription in the NHS**   **107**
Public policy context   107
Research problems   110
The partnership agreement   112
Partnership in practice? The employees' voice   116
Direct employee participation   117
Indirect employee participation   123
Union representation   125
Conclusion   129

6 **Goodbye Blue Sky: Partnership in the UK Aerospace Sector** **132**
Airframes and JetCo   136
Restructuring and financial control: The case of Airframes 137
Restructuring and financial control: The case of JetCo 142
Informal workplace partnership: The case of Airframes   147
Formal workplace partnership: The case of JetCo   153
Conclusion   162

7 **Whither Partnership?**   **165**
Consensus, consultation and ideology   167
Partnership and reality transcendence   170

Notes   176

References   178

Index   191

Figures

Figure 3.1   The recent consolidation of TUC affiliate unions   57
              in the finance sector
Figure 6.1   Major European aerospace and defence   135
              cross-holdings (Source: SBAC, 2003)

Tables

All organisations

Table 1.1	TUC principles of partnership	8
Table 2.1	Incidence of HPWS and partnership in six organisations	24
Table 2.2	Worker characteristics	26
Table 2.3	Change in job requirements and work intensity, by occupational class	28
Table 2.4	Change in job requirements and work intensity, by gender and contract	29
Table 2.5	High task discretion, by sector and occupational class	32
Table 2.6	Characteristics associated with task discretion	33
Table 2.7	Patterns of job satisfaction, by sector and occupational class	35
Table 2.8	Characteristics associated with job satisfaction	36
Table 2.9	Indicators of organisational commitment	38
Table 2.10	Characteristics associated with employee commitment	40
Table 2.11	Employees' assessment of the extent of direct consultation, by sector and occupational class	42
Table 2.12	Characteristics associated with consultation	43
Table 2.13	Workplace stress patterns, by sector and occupational class	45
Table 2.14	Characteristics associated with workplace stress	47
Table 2.15	Trade union members' assessment of union influence and performance, by sector	49
Table 2.16	Characteristics associated with union performance (union members only)	50

Finance organisations

Table 3.1	Employees' assessment of changes in skill level in recent years, all respondents	63
Table 3.2	Employees' experience of work intensification, all respondents	64

Table 3.3   Employees' assessment of the extent of direct   70
              communications and involvement
Table 3.4   Employees' assessment of partners' council/trade   75
              union influence at the workplace
Table 3.5   Employees' evaluation of who best represents them   79

Local authority

Table 4.1   CityCo's employees' views (excluding managers)   95
              on job security: Comparison between Best-Valued
              and non-Best-Valued departments
Table 4.2   Employees' experience (excluding managers) of work   99
              intensification at CityCo: Comparison between
              Best-Valued and non-Best-Valued departments
Table 4.3   Employee job satisfaction (excluding managers):   99
              Comparison between Best-Valued and
              non-Best-Valued departments
Table 4.4   Employees' evaluation (excluding managers) of how   101
              good managers are at employee communications
              and involvement: Comparison between Best-Valued
              and non-Best-Valued departments

NHS

Table 5.1   Employees' experience of work intensification   119
              and extensification in the past three years,
              by occupational group
Table 5.2   Employees' evaluation of managers' performance   121
              in respect to employee communications and
              involvement, by occupation group
Table 5.3   Employees' evaluation of the state of employee   126
              relations, by occupational group
Table 5.4   Union and non-union members' views of who best   128
              represents them in dealing with management
              about different workplace issues

Notes on the Authors

Andy Danford is Professor of Employment Relations at the Centre for Employment Studies Research, University of the West of England. He is the author of a number of books and journal articles on the themes of trade union renewal and critical studies of lean production and the high-performance workplace.

Mike Richardson is Senior Lecturer in Employee Relations at the University of the West of England, Bristol. His research interests include labour history, industrial sociology and the labour process. His recent publications include Richardson, M. (2006) 'Rapprochement and Retribution: The Divergent Experiences of Workers in Two Large Paper and Print Companies in the 1926 General Strike', *Historical Studies in Industrial Relations*, No. 22, 27–52.

Stephanie Tailby is Professor of Employment Studies at the University of the West of England, Bristol, and is Director of the Centre for Employment Studies Research. Her other recent research focuses on the contingent workforce in the healthcare and finance industries.

Martin Upchurch is Professor of International Employment Relations at Middlesex University Business School, London, where he convenes the Global Work and Employment Project. As well as writing and researching on UK industrial relations, he has authored articles on labour-related issues in Germany and the former Yugoslavia. His jointly authored book *The Crisis of Social Democratic Trade Unionism in Western Europe* is published by Ashgate in 2008.

Other books by the authors are *New Unions, New Workplaces: A Study of Union Resilience in the Restructured Workplace* (Routledge, 2003) and *Partnership and the High Performance Workplace: Work and Employment Relations in the Aerospace Industry* (Palgrave Macmillan, 2005).

Acknowledgements

The research for the book was funded with a grant from the ESRC Future of Work Programme: L212252096.

The authors would like to thank the managers, trade union representatives and employees who participated in our surveys and interviews. We would also like to thank Professor Peter Nolan, Director of the Future of Work programme, for his support and encouragement. Professor Paul Stewart of Strathclyde University also participated in some of the data collection and gave helpful advice. Viv Calway and Detta Danford also kindly helped with the transcribing of our mass of interview tapes.

1
Partnership at Work

This book results from a project funded by ESRC (Economic and Social Research Council) on the 'Patterns and Prospects of Partnership at Work in the UK'. The research project, conducted between 2001 and 2005, is part of the ESRC's 'Future of Work' programme. The project aimed to examine in detail the realities of partnership working in UK industry. Four chosen sectors – aerospace, finance, local government and health provided a total of six case study organisations, all with elements of partnership working apparent to a greater or lesser degree. A number of publications by the authors have already appeared focusing on one or other case study or sector, or on themes associated with partnership crossing one or more organisations or sectors. A sister book, *Partnership and the High Performance Workplace: Work and Employment Relations in the Aerospace Industry* (2005), has already been published in this same book series. This book brings together the major findings from six case studies.

What is partnership?

Partnership at Work is an illusive concept. Guest and Peccei (2001) expressed their difficulty in analysing partnership agreements when 'there is no agreed definition', while Oxenbridge and Brown (2004a) suggest that the term is 'too diffuse to carry much meaning'. Any attempt to define it might consequently be questioned by others who have a different idea of the concept. Despite this certainty of uncertainty we can hopefully offer some insights.

Consultation

First, the gathered evidence indicates that within the industrial relations process partnership emphasises the value of consultation at the expense of negotiation. In their evaluation of the government's Partnership at Work Fund, Terry and Smith (2003, p. 9) conclude:

> In organisations where trade unions were recognized the partnership initiative often involved a change in the structures through which unions and management interacted. Such changes were almost universally associated with an intention, explicit or otherwise, to change the dominant interaction between management and trade unions from one based around negotiation into one characterised as consultation.

The two types of relationship (consultation and negotiation) between employers and their staff are often presented as part of a spectrum, with consultation at one end implying information dissemination and opportunity for discussion, and negotiation at the other implying adversarial bargaining between formal representatives of the 'two sides of industry'. In reality, consultation is a top-down activity engendered by the employer, and negotiation is joint regulation between interest groups. This is not to say that negotiation is symbolic of perpetual workplace conflict. As Bélanger and Edwards (2007) have recently restated, workplace relations are a mixture of conflict and cooperation. Negotiation may be utilised by employers to legitimise their control beneath a veneer of representative democracy. Nevertheless negotiation does imply a pluralist intent, giving due regard to separate interests, while consultation has a neo-unitarist flavour, whereby management dominates the process. Negotiation is the traditional way in which unions have engaged with employers over distributive concerns, whereas consultation implies a softer employee relations strategy, integrative rather than distributive and able to take place with or without unions. An emphasis on consultation also implies a weakening of the collective ability of the workforce to be combative and oppositional to the employer. This is because negotiation is bound up with procedural activities (disputes and grievance procedures) that institutionalise 'them and us' in the workplace. Negotiation also implies the possibility of 'third party' interference from trade union full-time officials or from mediating bodies should negotiations break down with 'failure to agree'. In contrast, consultation remains an 'in-house' event, subject to more stringent ground rules of confidentiality and framed by the formal departmental structures of the organisation rather than the exigencies of employee representation within the industry. Finally, this preference in consultation for 'in-house' mechanisms and processes precludes the development of external worker solidarities within craft, occupation or industry that inform negotiation. We can thus sense in partnership a shift of power towards the employer, and this is confirmed with the second aspect of partnership – the preference for consensus at the expense of conflict.

Consensus

For consensus to be present it requires cross-table agreement and willingness to suppress dissent. It is an alternative method of resolving conflict at work to adversarialism. Advocates of partnership and high performance from the North American tradition such as Kochan and Osterman (1994) and Appelbaum et al. (2000) present it as an expression of mutuality of interest between employer and employee. Mutuality of interest is argued to be beneficial to both organisational competitiveness and employee welfare, in that the resulting productivity coalition between management and employees will give the worker greater job security. Partnership working is also presented by its advocates as a route to shared decision making, whereby workers may gain more job satisfaction and the organisation can benefit from workers' creative abilities and knowledge of the job in hand (see our earlier volume *Partnership and the High Performance Workplace*, for a review of this approach). This is the message contained in government publications supporting partnership and high performance working (DTI, 2002, 2004). However, if consensus is promoted as nirvana, then lingering conflict in the workplace is likely to be problematic. In such cases employers may seek to deinstitutionalise any pre-existing structures of conflict resolution as a precursor to partnership. Partnership may even be constructed by the employer as a method of substituting for or repressing collective identity and trade union attachment. In related fashion, employer insistence on consensus might have a utopian implication, whereby really existing conflict is denied in the pursuit of unrealistic consensus. Such reality transcendence can only be achieved by challenging existing sets of values and beliefs long imbued in the UK with 'them and us' adversarialism. For this reason we must acknowledge that there is a third dimension of partnership that is ideological and that seeks to transform British industrial relations in the name of 'modernisation'. It is to the New Labour Government that this task of ideological reshaping has fallen.

Ideology

The government's view of what partnership at work should achieve was outlined by Tony Blair when as prime minister he introduced the government's 1998 Fairness at Work document. Mr. Blair is worth quoting to help us understand New Labour's view of partnership:

> This White Paper is part of the Government's programme to replace the notion of conflict between employers and employees with the promotion of partnership. ... The White Paper steers a way between the absence of minimum standards of protection at the workplace, and a return to the laws of the past. It is based on the rights of the individual, whether exercised on their own or with others, as a matter of their choice. It matches rights and responsibilities. It seeks to draw a line under the issue of industrial relations law. There will be no going back. The days of strikes without ballots, mass picketing, closed shops and secondary action are over. Even after the changes we propose, Britain will have the most lightly regulated labour market of any leading economy in the world.... It is nothing less than to change the culture of relations in and at work – and to reflect a new relationship between work and family life. ... Already modern and successful companies draw their success from the existence and development of partnership at work. Those who have learnt to cherish and foster the creativity of their whole workforce have found a resource of innovation and inventiveness that drives their companies forward as well as enriching their lives. So the new culture we want to nurture and spread is one of voluntary understanding and co-operation because it has been recognised that the prosperity of each is bound up in the prosperity of all.
>
> (Blair in DTI (1998) foreword)

Despite New Labour's contemporary praise for partnership we need to recognise that antecedents had already begun to develop in the 1980s under Conservative governments in the guise of the 'single union deal' version of business unionism. The 'new realist' turn that many unions made in the 1980s was a defensive response to the on-slaught launched by the Thatcher governments. Inter-union disputes over single-union sweetheart deals had left a bad taste in the mouth of the Trades Union Congress (TUC) and its affiliates, and this par-ticular form of business unionism fell into disrepute (McIlroy, 1995, pp. 215–19). Notwithstanding these difficulties, partnership at work became a central theme of New Labour, indicating some continuity with the previous experiment. Partnership has been encouraged through a variety of government initiatives, including the establish-ment of a Partnership Fund for new employee–employer projects and legislative impetus for the establishment of workplace-based Union Learning Representatives, with the remit of creating up-skilling through training. The government introduced its Best Value 'modernisation' programme in the public sector within a partnership framework, and has sought to discuss general public sector 'reform' with trade unions within the Cabinet Office's *Drive for Change* initiative established in 2004 (www.driveforchange.org.uk). Impetus has also come from European Union-based initiatives such as the European Works Council Directive and the Information and Consultation Regulations, which prescribe consultative arrangements at the workplace. But despite all the attention, the number of recorded partnership deals is actually quite small.[1] The database of the Involvement and Participation Association (IPA) records no more than 150 such deals.[2] In reviewing the gathered evidence Bacon and Samuel (2007) record just 219 formal agreements signed from 1990 onwards. Gall (2004) finds that between 1995 and 2002 only 18 per cent of union recognition deals under the new legislation involved partnership arrangements. However, while the scope and extent of partnership may be small, fragmented and patchy, its significance lies in the fact that it has been jointly embraced by both employers and substantial sections of the trade union move-ment, including the TUC. A key purpose of this study is to understand why such interest has arisen, and in so doing to attempt to predict partnership's sustainability.

A new productive base?

We can locate New Labour interest in partnership within concern over the UK's continuing 'productivity gap' with competitor nations. Despite the restructuring of the UK's industrial base during the Con-servative years, the productivity gap between the UK and its major competitors remained. Rubery (1994) described the British economy in the late 1990s as a 'low wage, low skill economy, unable to compete in or effectively adjust to the demands of new international competition'. For New Labour in 1997 a different approach was needed (see Porter, 2003). The government produced a discussion paper on productivity in 2002, in which it stated:

> UK productivity remains lower than that of France and Germany, and substantially lower than that of the US – output per worker in the US is 38 per cent higher than in the UK, in France it is 18 per cent higher and in Germany 9 per cent higher. ... The productivity gap is due to a number of factors. One of these is the relative failure to invest in the skills and abilities of the workforce ... the Government believes productivity can be boosted by firms and employees working together to build high performance workplaces. The characteristics of high performance workplaces are high levels of adaptability, flexibility and involvement by both employees and employers. ... Information and consultation can be one of the ingredients of a modern, high performance workplace.
>
> (DTI, 2002)

As both Hay (2004) and Coats (2007) have observed, New Labour's approach transmuted into the dual objective of credibility in financial markets and competitiveness in the productive economy. The productivity problem could be addressed by focussing on organisational efficiency (Budd, 2004), with some concession to employee voice through partnership to ensure the 'progressive consensus in the workplace' espoused by Blair. This approach assumes that risks in the international product market can be minimised by adopting supply-side solutions to market problems (Thompson, 1996; Green et al., 2001). The strategy involved a drive both to increase labour market flexibility and to upgrade human capital through education and skills training under the aegis of Gordon Brown's 'post neo-classical endogenous growth theory'. The model is consistently presented as progressive and necessary in a globalised economy. It corresponds to wider moves spurred by the UK government in the EU, culminating in the agenda of the Lisbon Summit in 2000.

What is interesting about the new discourse from New Labour is that the peak organisations within industry, including the Confederation of British Industry (CBI) and TUC, as well as the Chartered Institute of Personnel and Development (CIPD) and Engineering Employers' Federation (EEF), rapidly took on the project. The Department of Trade and Industry (DTI) discussion paper was prepared in the light of earlier responses to the government's Productivity Initiative from the EEF and from a joint paper produced by the TUC and CBI. The EEF had commissioned its own study of the productivity gap in manufacturing between the USA and the UK (EEF, 2001). Called *Catching Up with Uncle Sam*, it extolled the virtues of skill enhancement as a tool 'to overcome barriers to investment, and the uptake of lean manufacturing'.[3] The TUC/CBI submission (TUC/CBI, 2001) took up the same themes stating that 'management leadership and employee involvement are complementary features of the high performance/high commitment model'. Further support came from a joint EEF/CIPD Report (2003) which identified workplace practices that could be identified with the HPWS and that have implications for the organisation of work as well as HR practice. They included many aspects associated with workplace flexibility and teamwork including work improvement teams and job redesign, as well as 'employee autonomy and involvement in decision-making'.

The high-performance manufacturing paradigm is not, however, the only source of government interest in partnership. In the public sector the Best Value 'modernisation' programme was also introduced under the rubric of partnership with staff and unions (Geddes, 2001; Whitfield, 2001; Richardson et al., 2005). Indeed, since 2001, the majority of partnership agreements signed have been in the public sector (Bacon and Samuel, 2007). In financial services the shift to an increasingly competitive environment has also created opportunities for employers to introduce work flexibility and performance agendas (Danford et al., 2003, pp. 97–121). Gall (1999, 2001) and Kelly (2005) note that there has been a sharp increase in partnership agreements utilised by employers in the banking industry as an attempt to countermobilise against the rise of union adversarialism.

The TUC and partnership

Within the new tripartite alliance on partnership, the position of the TUC deserves some further commentary. We can see that the TUC's support for partnership is focused on the contribution employee voice may make to organisational performance. The TUC's position was outlined in its response to the DTI Discussion Paper in 2002 (this time divorcing itself from the CBI). Citing evidence from academic studies and surveys, the TUC report stated:

> Engaging the expertise and knowledge of workers will help to ensure that bad judgements are avoided – and as a consequence, the legitimacy of the outcome is enhanced. It is important to recognise that while differences of interest between employers and workers are inevitable there are many areas where interests are shared. This fundamental principle must be understood if change is to be managed successfully and if more organisations in the UK are to become high performance workplaces.
>
> (TUC, 2002)

The embrace of partnership also had a strategic intent, reflecting its desire to once more be seen as a legitimate social and political actor, and in doing so the TUC has consistently sought to draw upon the labour-friendly institutional implications of the 'European Social Model'. This has sometimes placed the TUC at odds with the New Labour government, acting as critic when the government opposed or dragged its heels over the EU's worker consultation initiatives and labour-friendly aspects of the EU's Charter of Fundamental Rights. In other words, TUC support for partnership was not at any cost, and the TUC has sought to differentiate between what it sees as 'good' rather than 'bad' partnerships. Six principles of partnership were devised by the TUC (see Table 1.1) as an expression of the nature of 'good' as opposed to 'bad' partnership practice (TUC, 1999, 2002).

Table 1.1 TUC principles of partnership

- First, a joint commitment to the success of the enterprise.
- Second, unions and employers recognising each other's legitimate interests and resolving difference in an atmosphere of trust.
- Third, a commitment to employment security.
- Fourth, a focus on the quality of working life.
- Fifth, transparency and sharing information.
- Sixth, mutual gains for unions and employers, delivering concrete improvements to business performance, terms and conditions and employee involvement.

There is an emphasis on the necessity of independent trade unions to foster effective employee voice as well as reference to the 'mutual gains' inherent in the American Model. This is in contrast to the 1980s New Realist alternative strategy of the TUC which promoted collaborative concepts of business unionism and which Kelly (2005) has described as 'first generation' partnership. The TUC also emphasises the job security and trust aspects of high performance. In 2000, John Monks, then General Secretary of the TUC, stated:

> To create a real spirit of partnership – we found it essential to have a commitment to employment security. We all know and accept that employment levels in any enterprise can fall as well as rise. But we cannot expect people to commit themselves wholeheartedly to an organisation without any reciprocal commitment. Genuine partnership requires a trade-off between employee flexibility and security of employment. No employer could ever realistically guarantee that there would never be compulsory redundancies, but he or she could and should make it clear that this would be the last resort, and not the first response to a crisis.
>
> (Monks, 2000)

In 2002 the TUC surveyed evidence from 46 companies utilising its Partnership Institute and commented on the claimed link between partnership and performance, concluding that 'partnership workplaces are one-third more likely to have financial performance that is a lot better than average; and are a quarter more likely to have labour productivity that is a lot better than average' (TUC, 2002). Crucially, the Partnership Institute sought to draw the link between high-commitment management practices, high performance and a strong recognised union.[4] The emphasis on a 'strong' union creates space for the TUC to define a difference between 'good' partnerships and 'bad', without specifically defining what 'strong' trade unions means in practice. 'Good' partnership deals or agreements presumably not only achieve the six principles but are underpinned by union independence at the workplace, while 'bad' partnership deals fall short of the criteria and would not be supported by the TUC.[5] With this distinction between good and bad in mind, it should be noted that some employers may wish to introduce partnership arrangements not so much as a 'high road' route to competitiveness, but rather as a 'survival strategy' by which concessions can be gained from unions as an alternative to the threat of workplace closure (Heery, 2002). Following Crouch (1992), such arrangements have been labelled 'employer dominant' by Kelly (2005). They stand in contrast to arrangements which might arise when the union is well established, when the enterprise is well placed in the product market and the labour market is tight. In these circumstances it would be expected that the bargaining power of the workforce expressed through the union is high, and in consequence some degree of 'good' partnership might be achievable. Such points are also made by Jenkins (2007), when she correctly argues that in order to unpick the pros and cons of partnership we must first understand the organisational context in which it has been introduced.

However, when examining partnership arrangements introduced alongside new recognition deals, Gall (2004) finds that only a small proportion of self-styled partnership arrangements would fulfil the TUC's criteria for 'good' partnership. To counter such negative evidence, the TUC assumes that it is possible to achieve its six principles if the underlying conditions for 'good' partnership' are in place. According to the TUC, such underlying conditions may be absent due to unfavourable profiles of corporate governance, reflecting the general critiques of 'short-termism' and shareholder benefit at the expense of 'stakeholders' outside of the boardroom.[6] Counterarguments for a refined form of company pluralism have been set out by the TUC's Stakeholder Task Group, where TUC Policy Officer Janet Williamson argued for a company web of stakeholder interests, 'each of which is based on mutual dependence' (Williamson, 1997). Good partnership practice would thus sit side by side with 'good' corporate governance. What has emerged is a triple alliance between New Labour, employers and the TUC on the value of high-performance work systems and employee involvement. Differences exist within the alliance on the role and emphasis that should be placed on employee representation, but there is nevertheless an implicit commitment by the employers to recognise the value of employee voice (at least in some form) as a potential vehicle for enhancing creativity and innovation within the workplace.

Partnership as a 'Third Way' project

As we have already argued, the shift from conflict to 'progressive consensus in the workplace' cannot be achieved or sustained without reshaping the cultural landscape of British industrial relations. This is a question of a battle of ideas and attitudes in which New Labour has enlisted the ideology of the 'Third Way' (TW). Of course, experiments in union–employer collaboration have occurred before in British industrial relations. The Mond–Turner agreements of the late 1920s occurred in the aftermath of a major defeat for unions in the 1926 General Strike. There was a relatively closed economy, and the purpose was to press home employers' bargaining advantage and neutralise the resurgence of class struggle. The industrial democracy in the 1970s was an attempt to placate union demands for more organisational power, while the period of the social contract, in contrast, acted to contain rank-and-file wage militancy in the face of continuing balance of payments crises. Similarly, as Ramsay (1977, 1996) observed, employer interest in techniques of employee involvement was subject to cycles corresponding to periods of heightened industrial conflict, reaching a peak as employers seek to institutionalise and contain workers' increasing aspirations for workplace voice. We would contend that modern-day partnership, while reflecting some aspects of earlier experiences, is essentially a means by which collective labour strength is suppressed in the interest of business efficiency. We discern that while concessions have been made by New Labour in terms of the creation of a minimum wage and individual labour protection at work, the core values of the Conservative-era anti-union legislation have been preserved. New Labour remains hostile to EU legislation designed to re-enforce collective labour rights and refuses to provide institutional or legislative backing to social partnership *à la* European Social Model. In embracing the high-performance paradigm, the government then addresses workplace conflict over substantive issues through the lens of collaborative productivity coalitions between employers and employees.

An insight into this TW approach is provided by Martínez Lucio and Stuart (2005). In describing partnership at work as 'new industrial relations in a risk society', they equate the partnership discourse to the concepts of risk introduced by Beck (1992) and Giddens (1998) and suggest that partnership 'assumes a sharing of risk by capital and labour' in a 'marriage of convenience'. Contributions to the literature have also come from Ackers and Payne (1998) and Coats (2004), who regard partnership as an extension of pluralist principles within which trade unions can achieve new societal and workplace legitimacy.

Ackers (2002) and Ackers and Wilkinson (2003) develop the argument and make a plea to locate social partnership in terms of a 'neo-pluralist' framework, which they claim can provide a response to the threat of wider societal breakdown resulting from new forms of work and employment. Leaning on the sociology of Durkheim, they argue that there is a need for new normatively based institutions that can protect the citizen in an era of societal change and risk. Ackers (2002, p. 15) goes so far as to suggest that new institutional mechanisms associated with partnership can enable employers to make a 'constructive contribution to community and society'. This analysis argues that trade unions are subject to the perils of global competition but can redefine their role as protectors within society against the subsequent anomie. Coats (2004) expresses this point within a social capital framework, whereby he argues that trade unions are a source of both bridging and bonding social capital, implying a collective, collaborationist imperative with employers. Employers, too, are argued to be complicit in this new ideology, rejecting irresponsible and unethical exercise of power by multinational corporations in the global market (e.g. Giddens, 2000). The argument is that corporate power should be subject to voluntary restraint and moral imperative. Restraint is voluntary because anything statutory or regulatory might upset the market process. Alternatively, corporate power should be constrained by bringing the corporations into partnership with policy-makers within a new remit of corporate social responsibility. This is referenced by such initiatives as social and environmental audits, and a willingness of the corporation to engage more openly in public affairs in a progressive rather than regressive fashion (Prabhakar, 2003).

In this vein partnership is postulated in general UK government discourse on a variety of fronts beyond the workplace – between government and business but also between the agencies of state, markets and society in general (Catney, 2002). Partnership is even conceived as a form of 'new governance' typifying the ethic of the European Social Model (e.g. Kristensen, 2001), or as 'sustainable work systems' linked to a continuous regeneration of human resources (Docherty et al., 2002, p. 223). The suggestion that global restructuring of work is the precursor of new, more collaborative industrial relations is reinforced by other authors when considering the impact of EU legislation. Brown (2000), for example, suggests that global re-regulation is taking place, more inclusive of trade unions domestically and based on New Labour's commitment to developing partnership in practice. Brown constructs an institutional analysis by examining New Labour's domestic legislation, EU initiatives and developments in the 'social institutions' such as the Advisory, Conciliation and Arbitration Service (ACAS) and the Low Pay Commission. This is combined with a defensive change in UK trade unions towards 'a co-operative rather than a confrontational stance', which, according to Brown, means that 'social partnership appeared to be taking root' in the UK.

TW advocates produce the additional initiative of participatory democracy to cope with the excesses of global capitalism. The initiative is seen as an enabling mechanism by which the market can be constrained. It is this distinction which makes the TW different from the pure market imperative of neoliberalism. While there is no alternative (TINA) to the forces of globalization, it may be possible to use forms of ethical voluntarism to maintain social democratic values. Giddens relays the theme by suggesting:

> The left is defined by its concern with the dangers of [the] market, whose excesses need constantly to be reined back by the state. Today, however, this idea has become archaic. The left has to get comfortable with markets, with the role of business in the creation of wealth, and the fact that private capital is essential for investment.
>
> (1998, p. 34)

In adopting this philosophical approach New Labour cleared the ground for the abandonment of socialist critique of the market; and in so doing relegated workplace conflict to the sidelines. As the then Chancellor Gordon Brown told the CBI at their 1999 Conference, 'we must never again be seen as anti-success, anti-competition, anti-profit, anti-markets.' What remains is a form of 'ethical socialism' that gives priority to community over class: 'in which the S-word is retained but in its hyphenated form of social-ism' (Callinicos, 2001, p. 46). Part of this ethical approach includes new forms of participative and associative democracy, deemed necessary because of a decline of societal solidarity and a crisis of representative democracy (e.g. Cohen and Rogers, 1995). It is argued that this crisis is a cause of economic inefficiency, in that the negation of employee 'voice', combined with rising income inequality means that real solutions to real problems are less likely to be found within civil society. In other words, there is a link between the social institutions of capitalism and economic efficiency. In this vision old forms of representative democracy, associated with mass state provision of goods and services, are no longer appropriate to peoples' needs. The TW project becomes in essence Giddens's (2000) 'social investment state', whereby the role of the state mutates to one which discourages welfare dependency while providing incentives for personal advancement via education and training. Associative democracy, with horizontal networks of individuals acting as pressure within a renewed civil society, is presented as a more democratic framework designed to increase rates of social capital formation, participation and societal efficiency. Translated to the restructured workplace, the process of participation and partnership is again postulated as key to economic and production efficiency, either as pluralist networks of stakeholders in the corporation (Hirst, 1994, 1997; Kelly et al., 1997; Kelly and Parkinson, 2001) or, as Archer (1996) suggests, in terms of economic democracy expressed through Works Councils.

Critics from within and without

Academic comment on these debates has been voluminous, focusing on either the nature of partnership agreements, the processes involved in partnership or the cultural characteristics of partnership attached to the employer–employee relationship. Broadly speaking, academic dialogue can be characterised as contestation between those who might be labelled 'advocates' of partnership and those who are 'critics', although some, such as Heery (2002), might sit between the two camps. Advocates usually stress the benefits of employee voice and engagement with employers for organisational performance within the high-performance paradigm (e.g. Huselid, 1995; Black and Lynch, 2000, 2001; Michie and Sheehan, 2003), while others focus on the arguments for partnership as a necessary strategic reorientation for unions if they are to survive and thrive in an increasingly competitive environment (e.g. Haynes and Allen, 2001; Samuel, 2005). They are joined by those such as Ackers (2002) and Ackers and Wilkinson (2003) who have championed the 'new pluralist' vision of the role of trade unions. Both sets of authors represent a pessimistic view of the ability of trade unions to continue to progress through adversarialism.

The critics focus on the ambiguous or negative effects on company performance (Guest et al., 2003), or the deleterious outcomes for workers of partnership in the workplace. Such negative outcomes include a general intensification and extensification of work as employer flexibility agendas impact on the labour process (e.g. Taylor and Ramsay, 1998; Martínez Lucio and Stuart, 2002; Findlay and McKinlay, 2003). McIlroy describes the limitations of partnership in the face of neoliberal market imperatives and contends that New Labour has embraced the neoliberalism of its Conservative predecessor. He posits that far from introducing 'new pluralism', 'it [partnership] embraced a unitary framework of industrial relations and the rhetoric of human resource management' (McIlroy, 1998, p. 543). Such a theme is supported by Martínez Lucio and Stuart (2000), who suggest that partnership is simply an extension of 'tired' HRM and is an attempt by employers to reinvigorate processes of employee involvement whereby worker commitment to organisational goals can be used to increase worker productivity. In summary, partnership cannot be viewed outside the context of employer (and government) attempts to restructure industry and to increase worker productivity. As we argued in *Partnership and the High Performance Workplace* (Danford et al., 2005, p. 236) partnership and high-performance working 'cannot mask irreconcilable conflicts of interest that are prime characteristics of capitalist workplace dynamics'.

Much evidence from case study research would suggest that partnership has been highly divisive in the workplace. Workers and their unions are often divided, but what is notable in many cases of partnership is the *ideological* rather than sectional nature of division. Where partnership arrangements have been introduced they have also been found to create new divisions between senior union activists and the rank and file. The senior activists became either 'detached' from the membership (Marks et al., 1998; Danford et al., 2003) or 'displaced' (Geary and Roche, 2003). Such detachment derives largely from the emphasis on consultation that is prominent within partnership arrangements and agreements. The processes involved in negotiation codify the outcomes of bargaining power into transparent written agreements. In contrast, consultation decodifies arrangements between the parties. Partnership replaces traditional written agreements with informal, unwritten and consensus-based 'agreements'. The lack of formal codification in partnership thus produces 'agreements' between the union leaderships and employers which are less transparent and accountable to the rank and file than those previously produced under traditional bargaining structures. In addition, more business-related information is released to senior union activists and full-time union officials by the employer in the consultation/ partnership process, but this is often on a 'need to know' and confidential basis. Further division is created between 'information rich' senior workplace representatives and 'information poor' union members. The dangers of detachment may also occur where the union has sought to reach a partnership arrangement with the employer that trades employee compliance for union privilege in recruiting members. Such was the outcome in Heery et al.'s (2005) study of the Manpower staff agency, whereby 'an officer dependent, passive form of trade unionism has been viewed as a constraint upon, and not a condition for, the development of a broader exchange with the company' (ibid., p. 182). Most importantly the process of partnership also runs the risk of pacifying the rank and file (Blyton and Turnbull, 1998, p. 106). This is because the consensus nature of the process, when combined with detachment of the senior activists, can act to undermine activism and marginalise 'oppositionism' within the general membership. Employers' agendas to utilise partnership processes as a vehicle for the management of change have also necessitated the 'cultivation' of union activists who are sympathetic to the general project. In his study of Legal and General and Amicus-MSF, Samuel highlights how opposition to partnership was overcome by a group of union activists who 'were given extended reach into management decision-making'. These 'cultivated' activists then proceeded to enable the workplace union 'to exert pressure as the "conscience" of the company' (Samuel, 2005, p. 73). Lastly, we must record that the question of partnership can also divide workers in their workplaces both at the time when new partnership projects are conceived and also as the outcomes of the partnership agreements begin to emerge. Kelly (1999) refers to the opposition from stewards to partnership before it was introduced at Blue Circle, the 49 per cent vote against the introduction of partnership at Scottish Power and the initial rejection of partnership at United Distillers. Beale (2005) in the case of Inland Revenue, and Gall (2005) in the case of Royal Mail, also provide evidence of workers turning against partnership once the outcomes unravel and disappointment sets in.

New opposition?

Such ambivalence to the partnership agenda is rooted within ideo-logical differences in the trade unions at national level between New Labour values of 'modernisation' and Old Labour values of public service provision and industrial relations adversarialism. This disjuncture between government and union policy in the public sector has created a particular focus for the retention of partnership discourse by the TUC and public sector unions over the future of public service delivery in Britain. A 2003 TUC resolution referred to a 'spirit of partnership which needs to be adopted between government departments and agencies and the trade unions representing workers in these important and demanding public services'. However, the strains between unions and government on this issue are highlighted in the resolution's *caveat*:

> Congress urges those in government to enact their obligations under international law, and not seek to remove the ability of the trade unions to protect their members by the use of industrial action. The trade union movement demands of its 'political arm', the Labour Party, that all partnership agreements are enacted with the full backing of international law, and that these are partnerships of equals and do not demand trade unions to be 'silent partners'.
>
> (TUC, 2003)

Indeed, from a position of general support in the early years of the New Labour government, many in the union movement have now moved to a position of criticism. Robert Taylor concludes in his review of the evidence for the government-funded ESRC:

> The critics of partnership at work in Britain have certainly grown more widespread and influential in recent years. Their attacks have begun to exercise a significant influence over the attitude of pub-lic policy-makers towards the concept. Partnership has never been without its opponents who see it as an inappropriate means for developing new forms of industrial relations. Now it is finding it difficult to remain on any public policy agenda at all.
>
> (Taylor, 2004, p. 6)

This is not to say that there is outright opposition to partnership, but rather retreat to a position in which partnership is viewed merely as a possible tactical approach by employers who may be reluctant to deal with unions on other terms. Unions now hostile to partnership provide examples of this approach. Amicus (now part of UNITE), for example, signed a major partnership agreement in the print industry in 2005 through the DTI Strategic Partnership Fund. The agreement 'contains 12 key objectives such as increasing dialogue between employers, employees and their union, improving productivity, reducing excessive overtime working, assisting employees to adapt to change, and enabling effective recruitment and development of employees'. It also contained new provisions on key issues, such as sick pay, the regulation of agency and temporary workers, information and consultation, and flexible working patterns (*Personnel Today*, 2005). The CWU, whose left leadership is formally hostile to partnership, continues to sign partnership agreements with small employers on the fringe of the industry. General Secretary Billy Hayes outlined the tactic in this way: 'We actually have partnership agreements in some telecommunication firms, where we do not have full negotiating rights. We regard partnership agreements in these certain instances, as an interim measure on the way to more mature and respectful relationship between equals' (Hayes, 2006). Opposition to partnership has developed as more left-wing trade union leaders have emerged in recent years and as the outcomes of previous partnership arrangements have proved disappointing to the rank and file. The election of a 'broad left' leadership of the Public and Commercial Services Union (PCS) in 2003 is one such example, whereby the previous long-held support for partnership in principle has been reversed (Beale, 2005).

The studies

We attempt to address such debates as outlined in our assessment of the reality of workplace partnership. Our research project is grouped around case studies of partnership in four employment sectors: aerospace, finance, health and local government. In Chapter 2 we provide a presentation of statistical data from our surveys. The analysis investigates such variables as worker assessment of management performance in managing people; worker assessment of union performance; levels of worker autonomy, commitment and job satisfaction; and extent of job security, labour intensification and workplace stress. Nearly 2600 questionnaire returns from manual and non-manual employees were assessed, from which 1400 surveyed employees worked in a group governed by a partnership industrial relations framework, and 1200 worked in non-partnership areas. The research was carried out between 2001 and 2004 in workplaces based in the south-west of England. We see no significance in the choice of geographical region and have no reason to believe, given the heterogeneity of the chosen sectors, to find different results in any other region of the UK. Our workplaces reflect the diverse nature of employment in Britain and contain employees and unions at either end of and within the moderate–militant spectrum. In each subsequent chapter we examine case studies through a combination of document analysis, interviews with management and staff and surveys of employees. Our sectors represent different contexts for the study of partnership. In our two case studies in aerospace, we have found an emphasis on the high-performance work system, where partnership is integral to the process of introduction of new ways of working and ways of communicating. We have recorded our views in detail in our sister book *Partnership and the High Performance Workplace* (2005). In this book we review our arguments and compare the aerospace sector with our other examples. In finance we have chosen two case studies, one from the insurance industry and the other a former building society, now part of a larger banking organisation. These studies focus on different employer relations strategies in a rapidly changing competitive environment. One of our case studies is non-union, while the other is unionised, but with recent decline in union membership and density (see Upchurch et al., 2006; Tailby et al., 2007). Our case studies in health focus on two hospital trusts since merged into one and based a few miles apart from each other, but with different industrial relations environments and traditions. We focus in particular on the impact of partnership on gains and losses in employee voice and employee well-being and reflect on the government's modernisation agenda and its impact on the stakeholders within the NHS (see also Tailby et al., 2004). Finally, in local government, we focus on a large local authority which has been subject to the government's Best Value approach. We compare and contrast the experience of employees in two departments of the authority and record and analyse the effects of the partnership approach to the reform of public service delivery (see Richardson et al., 2005). Our final chapter attempts to draw together some conclusions and to provide some insights into future prospects for workplace partnership in the UK.

2
The High-Performance Workplace: Fact or Fiction?

Many accounts of the nature of the high-performance workplace (HPW) tend to derive from 'technologist' conceptions of industrial development. This often results in analyses that are neutral, or silent, on such questions as capitalist dynamics and class relations at work. For example, one of the leading groups of writers in the field, Eileen Appelbaum and her colleagues (Appelbaum et al., 2000), have argued that the antecedents of the HPW can be traced back to the team-based experiments associated with the human relations and group relations movements earlier in the last century. While much is made of the importance for 'progressive employers' of raising workers' discretionary effort through less authoritarian methods of managing labour, there is a certain reticence here in considering how these processes may serve to obscure the sources of labour exploitation at the point of production and service. This technologist emphasis is apparent again in the positioning of the emergence of the HPW in the context of shifting economic and market environments. Here the techno-economic features of globalisation are stressed, such as the geographical extensiveness and intensification of market competition along with associated technological developments and supports that include post-Fordist advances in product and service design and developments in ICT and flexible technologies (Appelbaum et al., 2000; Ashton and Sung, 2002; Brown and Lauder, 2001; White et al., 2004). For such writers, the implication for labour management is that these developments can create the conditions for the development of new high-skill employment strategies where 'high performance' employers offer their staff more rewarding, skilled work and greater job security in exchange for more effort and greater commitment to the organisation.

Such assumptions have been questioned from a number of different angles. For example, adopting a political economy of skill perspective, Lloyd and Payne (2006) have noted a tendency of writers to accept the high-performance model without being sufficiently clear about its theoretical or practical substance. There is also a problem of reification in that, despite evidence to the contrary, too many researchers assume that the implementation of the model will inevitably generate mutual gains for employers and workers in terms of labour productivity, skill content of jobs, employee satisfaction, autonomy and so on. Writing in a similar vein, Godard (2001, 2004) argues that without a radical transformation of the current institutional context of the HPW, any attempt to implement high-performance reforms will inevitably founder on the rocks of the exigencies of neoliberal capitalism: short-termism, cost control and profit maximisation. Since, under these conditions, the employment relationship can be seen more explicitly to be based on labour subordination (and a subordination of labour's interests to the employer's) then the inevitable low trust and interest conflict between managers and workers will render the HPW, based as it is on notions of high trust and mutual gain, somewhat problematic.

These criticisms have a good deal of congruence with the case study analysis presented in this book. What they don't address, however, is the question of how analysis of the roots of the HPW can provide important insights into the nature of the model and its potential contradictions. As already noted, Appelbaum et al. (2000) locate the HPW along a continuum of management initiative and ideology aimed at securing greater discretionary effort from workers without relying on the conventions of tight supervisory control and compulsion. An alternative continuum, and one with a shorter timescale, encompasses the similarity between the HPW and, what some writers regard as its progenitor, lean production. The two models share a good number of core management processes and labour deployment techniques, for instance, worker involvement in teams and kaizen, and integrative employee voice mechanisms such as direct consultation and cooperative trade union relations. Advocates of the HPW claim that what is new about their model is not the lean management techniques themselves but their clustering around coherent bundles of synergistic practices with a raft of supporting HRM practices. The assumption here is that various techniques centring on skill development, job redesign and employee and union participation may interact so that the sum effects on both workers' job satisfaction and organisational performance are stronger than the effects of individual practices (Batt and Appelbaum, 1995; Kochan and Osterman, 1994). In postulating this argument, and thereby setting up the HPW in contradistinction to lean production, such writers neatly sidestep a nagging problem. That is, in the light of a well established and sustained critique of the lean production model (see, for example, Danford, 1999; Delbridge, 1998; Elger and Smith, 2005; Head, 2003; Mehri, 2005; Nichols and Cam, 2005, Rinehart et al., 1997; Stewart et al., 2004), the idea that what is essentially a reformed version of lean can, nevertheless, generate much different outcomes seems somewhat questionable.

As we have argued previously (see Danford et al., 2005), lean production has rarely generated conditions for so-called worker 'empowerment'. Instead, in many cases it has resulted in a deterioration of workers' quality of working life in the form of job strain, work intensification, job insecurity and stress. The current interest in the HPW centres not just on the labour productivity advantages for the employer but equally on the 'mutual gain' that negates such deleterious worker outcomes. This, of course, is an argument that requires systematic empirical interrogation. But it does seem that part of the attraction of the HPW concept is that it constitutes a reply to the critics of lean and one that paves the way for further 'inevitable' organisational change on the employer's terms. That is, the more 'holistic' approach to work reform in the HPW is seen to overcome the contradictions of lean production and, in particular, the problems of deteriorating quality of working life while systematically raising workers' effort rates and productivity. As proposed initially by Appelbaum et al. (2000), the adoption by firms of high-performance management practices may set forth a process of interplay between material and psychological factors that generates higher-skilled workers with more satisfying jobs, in turn leading to more committed workers offering greater discretionary effort under conditions of lower workplace stress.

In different ways, the ideology of 'mutual gain' is critically evaluated in each of the organisational case study chapters in this book. This chapter helps set the context for our case study research by presenting systematic quantitative analysis of the questionnaire survey data collected from each of the six organisations, a merged dataset comprising 2577 responses. The chapter explores a broad range of themes that are central to the labour-centred HPW agenda:

- the nature of job recomposition (for example patterns of changing skills, job responsibilities and worker flexibility) and related patterns of work intensity
- the extent of workers' task discretion
- patterns of job satisfaction and worker commitment to the organisation
- workers' assessment of staff consultation outcomes
- the extent of workplace stress
- workers' assessment of union performance

As well as presenting overall trends, the analysis will highlight differences in worker experience in high-performance work settings and thus question the implicit assumption that high-performance work reforms engender mutual gains for all workers in unitary fashion. Specifically, we test for any differences in outcomes on the basis of sociological characteristics such as occupational class, gender, ethnicity and age, along with additional factors such as employment contract, length of service and union membership.

High-performance work practices and worker attributes

The six case study organisations had each adopted a relatively large number of high-performance work techniques, known in the literature as high-performance work systems (HPWS). A summary is provided in Table 2.1. Every organisation had adopted a form of self-directed teams where members had a degree of autonomy over questions of job priorities and staff deployment. This form of work design was not used uniformly across each establishment, however. Around half of the workers surveyed were deployed in these teams, varying from 44 per cent at JetCo to 62 per cent at FinanceCo. One manifestation of labour flexibility was the use of job rotation within teams in all establishments and staff rotation between teams at all organisations except the aerospace firms. With the exception of the local authority CityCo, integrated project teams were also used as forums for non-manual staff participation in team-based discussions on project and design issues and production/service problems. Quality circles and other types of

Table 2.1 Incidence of HPWS and partnership in six organisations

	Aerospace JetCo	Aerospace Airframes	Finance FinanceCo	Insurance InsuranceCo	Local Authority CityCo	NHS Trust GH Trust
Self-directed teams	Yes	Yes	Yes	Yes	Yes	Yes
Integrated project teams	Yes	Yes	Yes	Yes	No	Yes
Problem-solving groups	Yes	Yes	Yes	Yes	Yes	Yes
Job rotation within teams	Yes	Yes	Yes	Yes	Yes	Yes
Job rotation between teams	No	No	Yes	Yes	Yes	Yes
Team briefing	Yes	Yes	Yes	Yes	Yes	Yes
Formal consultation practices	Yes	Yes	Yes	Yes	Yes	Yes
Works Council/Cons Comm	Yes	Yes	Yes	Yes	Yes	Yes
Attitude surveys	Yes	Yes	Yes	Yes	Yes	Yes
Employee appraisals	Yes	Yes	Yes	Yes	Yes	Yes
Off-the-job training	Yes	Yes	Yes	Yes	Yes	Yes
On-the-job training	Yes	Yes	Yes	Yes	Yes	Yes
Merit/incentive pay	Yes	No	Yes	Yes	No	No
Share ownership scheme	Yes	Yes	No	No	No	No
Profit-sharing scheme	No	Yes	Yes	Yes	No	No
Harmonized conditions	Yes	Yes	Yes	Yes	Yes	Yes
Partnership	Only Non-manuals	Only Manuals	Yes	Yes	No	Yes

problem-solving groups were also in use in each organisation and again participation rates varied (from 16 per cent in General Hospital Trust to 69 per cent in InsuranceCo).

There was a greater pattern of uniformity in the provision of 'employee voice' mechanisms. All employees in every establishment received regular team briefings and communication cascades from their supervisors. They were also subject to other direct consultation techniques such as attitude surveys and group meetings with directors ('town hall' meetings). All were represented by elected employees or union stewards on company councils (in the case of the aerospace and finance and insurance firms) or on corporate-level joint consultative committees in the case of the two public sector organisations. As far as complementary HRM practices are concerned, and training and development in particular, each of the six organisations operated appraisal systems for all their employees. They also offered relatively generous formal and informal skills training (although the more expensive and time-consuming training packages tended to be skewed towards managers and graduates). As for pay and conditions, all six organisations offered competitive pay rates within their own sectors along with harmonised conditions; three out of the four private sector organisations included merit pay and profit-related bonuses in their remuneration packages and two provided employee share ownership schemes.

As the case study chapters describe in more detail, a significant number of workers surveyed were based in establishments or departments that were subject to the development of partnership relationships between management and employee representatives. In three cases, partnership framework agreements were in place (FinanceCo, InsuranceCo and the non-manual bargaining group in JetCo). In FinanceCo (the only non-union firm in the sample) partnership working was embodied in the operation of a Partners Council, a joint committee of elected staff representatives including a full time representative. In InsuranceCo, and for the non-manual group in JetCo, agreements emphasising 'collaborative' union–management relationships existed. These offered involvement in joint management–union working parties and other management forums in return for union commitment to organisational goals. In two more cases (the manual bargaining group in the second aerospace firm, Airframes, and the General Hospital Trust), management had developed new partnership environments. Management policy in these areas was to explicitly promote joint-working and more extensive union involvement in strategic plans and operational matters via existing bargaining and consultative machinery. In the remaining cases (CityCo, manual workers in JetCo and non-manual workers in Airframes), traditional bargaining relations obtained. In CityCo, apart from local pilot initiatives in a few departments, management had made no attempt to introduce partnership as a corporate policy. In the aerospace firms these occupational bargaining groups had rejected management overtures to partnership and had adopted conventional – and at times militant – organising strategies. Across the six establishments, 1374 of the workers surveyed were based in a partnership environment while the other 1202 were not.

The characteristics of the survey respondents are summarised in Table 2.2. The overall patterns disguise a number of differences within the six workplaces. For example, the workforces tended to be younger in FinanceCo and InsuranceCo. Equally, the gender balance

Table 2.2 Worker characteristics

	(N)	(%)
Women	883	34
Men	1688	66
Black & Minority Ethnic (BME)	98	4
Permanent	2452	96
Temporary/agency	108	4
Line managers	390	15
Graduate staff	241	9
Non-graduate technical/specialists	697	27
Admin staff & clerical	395	15
Skilled manuals	634	25
Semi-skilled/unskilled manuals	205	8
Age: 24 years or less	177	7
Age: 25–29 years	285	11
Age: 30–39 years	692	27
Age: 40–49 years	775	30
Age: 50 years or more	634	25
Length of service: less than 2 years	275	11
Length of service: 2 to < 5 years	641	25
Length of service: 5 to < 10 years	380	15
Length of service: 10 years or more	1265	49

Note: n = 2577.

was skewed towards men in the two aerospace firms and towards women in General Hospital Trust, FinanceCo and InsuranceCo.

Work intensity and job recomposition

National and international surveys of employees' quality of working life have provided compelling evidence that effort rates increased steadily during the 1980s and 1990s (Burchell, 2002; Gallie et al., 1998; Green 2001 and 2006). Green (2006) has provided the most comprehensive and rigorous analysis of this trend. Drawing on a range of datasets, he describes clear patterns of labour intensification during the 1980s and most of the 1990s with large proportions of workers – particularly managers and professionals – reporting the need to work at high speed and exerting greater effort as a result of both job pressures and discretionary effort. Green notes a range of contributory factors. These include the rising demands of the customer or client, the impact of peer pressure and workers' individual discretion. But the most consistent underlying factor is technological change in the form of both new technologies and new ways of organising work. His survey evidence suggests also that while work intensity remained high it reached apparent satiation after 1997. This corresponds with the recent results of the UK Workplace Employment Relations Surveys. These have shown high levels of work intensity across a broad range of sectors and workplaces but no change in employee assessments of intensity between 1998 and 2004 (Cully et al., 1999; Kersley et al., 2006).

Our case study survey results and interviews also suggested a high degree of work intensity. Unlike the recent national trends, however, they showed that effort rates in the six high-performance work organisations continued to increase. In Tables 2.3 and 2.4 we present the results for a number of questions related to changes in work intensity and job composition over the three-year period leading up to the research (from 1999 to 2002–3). Large proportions of workers reported increases in the amount of work they were expected to complete each week. Although this was higher for line managers the data did not indicate an obvious divide between non-manual and manual workers. Another dimension of work intensification is extensive effort, relating to an increase in working hours. In the light of a long-term decline in average weekly work hours in the UK (Green, 2001) it is notable that

Table 2.3 Change in job requirements and work intensity, by occupational class

	Line managers (%)	Graduate staff (%)	Technical/ specialist (%)	Admin staff (%)	Skilled manual (%)	Semi-/ unskilled (%)
Increase in amount of work expected to complete each week	73	57	66	60	55	67
Increase in number of hours expected to work in a typical week	37	24	20	18	17	16
Increase in responsibility involved in job	82	73	72	62	60	57
Increase in skill level required for job	74	62	70	63	47	45
Increase in degree of flexibility required in job	77	63	70	60	76	65

Table 2.4 Change in job requirements and work intensity, by gender and contract

	Male workers	Female workers	Permanent contract workers	Temporary contract workers	Agency workers
Increase in amount of work expected to complete each week	61	65	64	41	33
Increase in number of hours expected to work in a typical week	20	26	22	16	11
Increase in responsibility involved in job	67	70	69	67	44
Increase in skill level required for job	59	64	61	57	57
Increase in degree of flexibility required in job	74	60	70	49	57

a significant minority of workers in our survey reported an increase in hours over the three-year period. However, unlike national trends there was not a particularly wide dispersion of hours in our case study samples. The mean average working week (including overtime) amounted to just over 39 hours and only 4 per cent worked 20 hours or less; only 6 per cent worked 48 hours or more.

Table 2.3 also shows that the job content of many of these workers had enlarged over the three-year reporting period. Large proportions of manual and non-manual workers indicated that the levels of responsibility and skill required in their jobs had increased as had the degree of flexibility. Again, the proportion of managers reporting this was higher but not significantly so. There were also a number of differences based on gender but no consistent pattern overall (Table 2.4). In addition, workers on permanent contracts were more likely to report enlarged job content and greater work intensity compared to those employed on temporary or agency contracts. This suggests that the work organisational changes and adoption of HPWS described in subsequent chapters of this book were centred more on the core workforces of the six establishments. This pattern of functional flexibility corresponds with both Atkinson's (1984) original model of the flexible organisation and Ackroyd and Procter's (1998) more recent formulation of the new flexible firm.

Additional bivariate analysis showed that increases in the amount of work expected to be completed each week were correlated with increases in responsibility, skill and flexibility, as were increases in hours. Pearson correlation coefficients were much higher in the case of increases in the amount of work suggesting that job recomposition, and associated work organisational change, were significant pressures on the patterns of intensive effort in the six organisations.

Task discretion

We now turn to the related factor of task discretion. It is an important theme in the HPW debate since the model assumes that workers should have considerable autonomy over how their jobs and tasks are organised and completed (Appelbaum et al., 2000). In this respect, task discretion is linked often to high levels of skill and trust since, if workers are to be expected to make decisions about their work and performance, then they should be trusted by management to do this, provided they possess the requisite problem-solving skills and knowledge (Gallie et al., 2004; Green, 2006). The evidence for recent trends in task discretion in UK workplaces is not auspicious, however. While national surveys have shown that task discretion is associated with higher occupational classes, there has been a decline in task discretion in the UK, particularly among professional workers (Gallie et al., 2004; Green, 2006).

Workers in our survey were asked how much influence they had both in deciding *what* tasks they completed and *how* they carried their tasks out. Also, they were asked how much influence their supervisors had in deciding both of these. We then created a composite measure for task discretion. Responses to the first two questions on personal control were coded as four (a lot), three (some), two (a little) and one (none). The same coding, in reverse order, was used for the second set of questions on supervisory control. This group of questions had an internal consistency reliability (Cronbach's alpha) of 0.672. A composite task discretion score was derived by adding the scores for the responses to each question and dividing by the number of questions (four).

In Table 2.5, we first present the findings governing the proportions of workers who indicated that they had 'a lot' of influence (equating with high task discretion). These suggest that discretion over how to complete the range of tasks in their jobs was relatively high (especially for line managers and graduates) but lower for decisions governing what tasks to complete. In other words, discretion was higher for task design but lower for task deployment.

At this point, and in subsequent sections in this chapter, we present OLS regression analysis to explore the interaction effects of different worker attribute variables and job recomposition variables. We had two main points of interest in performing this multivariate analysis. First, and in the context of the unitary mutual gain discourse of the HPW, we sought to explore the evidence that any high-performance outcomes are distributed equally across different groups of workers, such as those employed in different sectors, from different occupational groups, genders, employment contracts, age groups and so on. And, second, to assess the extent to which our key job recomposition and work intensity variables affected these outcomes. For task discretion, our results are presented in Table 2.6.

For the different worker groups, a number of patterns emerge. As far as occupational class is concerned, and using administrative staff

Table 2.5 High task discretion, by sector and occupational class

	A lot of personal influence over what tasks to complete (%)	A lot of personal influence over how to complete tasks (%)	A lot of supervisory influence over what tasks to complete (%)	A lot of supervisory influence over how to complete tasks (%)
Aerospace	26	50	28	8
NHS/Loc govt.	28	42	26	14
Finance	33	51	31	14
Line managers	59	76	12	4
Graduate staff	28	59	21	9
Technical/ Specialist staff	28	46	25	12
Admin staff	24	37	30	15
Skilled manual	15	41	37	7
Semi-skilled/ Unskilled manual	13	25	38	23

Table 2.6   Characteristics associated with task discretion

	Unstandardised beta coefficients	Significance
(Constant)	2.419	***
NHS/Loc govt (ref. Aero)	−0.031	
Finance	−0.066	
Line managers (ref. admin staff)	0.366	***
Graduate staff	0.297	***
Technical/Specialist staff	0.094	**
Skilled manual	−0.081	
Semi-skilled manual	−0.237	***
Male (ref. female)	−0.007	
BME (ref. White British)	−0.098	
< 2 years service (ref. > 10 years)	−0.130	**
2–5 years service	−0.031	
5–10 years service	0.013	
Age 16–24 years (ref. > 50 years)	−0.324	***
Age 25–29 years	−0.130	***
Age 30–39 years	−0.120	***
Age 40–49 years	−0.063	*
Temporary worker (ref. permanent)	0.040	
Agency worker (ref. non-agency)	−0.176	*
Union member (ref. non-union)	−0.040	
Average weekly hours	0.006	***
Increase in responsibility	0.175	***
Increase in skill	−0.041	
Increase in flexibility	−0.017	
Increase in amount of work	0.035	
Increase in weekly hours	−0.018	
$R^2 = 0.137$		
N = 2213		

Note: *** = significant at 1% level ($p \leq 0.01$), ** = significant at 5% level ($p \leq 0.05$), * = significant at 10% level ($p \leq 0.10$).

as the reference group, the results show a link between class and task discretion. Discretion is significantly higher for non-manual and supervisory occupations and lower for manual workers (especially semi-skilled and unskilled workers). More predictably, every age group under 50 had significantly less discretion compared to those aged 50 and above. This suggests that while 'high performance' work organisation may influence task discretion, employees' age and work experience are equally important contributory factors. Lastly, the results show that while task discretion is quite predictably linked to increases in job responsibilities, it is also associated with higher working hours suggesting some tension in the relationship between discretion, autonomy and quality of working life in the six establishments. We return to this theme in some of our other models below.

Job satisfaction

The hypothetical link between job satisfaction and the use of HPWS is based on the assumption that workers are likely to value opportunities to participate in decision making at work, along with intrinsic job rewards such as interesting work and good management relations, and material incentives such as higher pay (Appelbaum et al., 2000). Moreover, implicit in the HPW model is the assumption that mutual gain benefits such as higher job satisfaction are felt by all workers in an organisation (Appelbaum et al., 2000; Ashton and Sung, 2002; Rothschild, 2000). To explore this, our questionnaire survey asked four questions related to satisfaction. Three were linked to qualitative, relational facets of work and a fourth concerned material reward. The first three concerned satisfaction with the amount of influence employees had over their job, with the sense of achievement they got from their work, and with the respect they got from supervisors/line managers. The fourth covered satisfaction with the amount of pay received. Coded from one to four (very dissatisfied to very satisfied) we used the same procedure followed for task discretion to derive a composite job satisfaction score. The questions had an internal consistency reliability (Cronbach's alpha) of 0.682.

Table 2.7 indicates that overall satisfaction with the three qualitative dimensions of work was relatively high (particularly in the finance sector companies) but that satisfaction with pay was much lower. There was also an occupational effect in that satisfaction rates were lower for the two manual worker groups, particularly governing respect received from supervisors and pay satisfaction. The discrepancy between satisfaction with the three qualitative aspects of work and satisfaction with pay is important because, as recent analysis of job satisfaction patterns in the UK has found, many workers, in fact, tend to prioritise pay and conditions over the more intrinsic elements of work. That is, they rate satisfaction with a job higher than satisfaction with their work (Rose, 2003, p. 505). If this is the case, then overall satisfaction

Table 2.7 Patterns of job satisfaction, by sector and occupational class

	Satisfied/ Very satisfied (%)	Dissatisfied/ Very dissatisfied (%)	Unsure (%)
The amount of influence you have over your job			
Aerospace	64	30	6
NHS/Loc govt	58	34	8
Finance	73	20	7
Line managers	76	20	4
Graduate staff	65	28	7
Technical/Specialist staff	62	32	6
Admin staff	63	29	8
Skilled manual	57	36	7
Semi-skilled/Unskilled manual	57	36	7
The sense of achievement you get from your work			
Aerospace	66	29	5
NHS/Loc govt	66	30	4
Finance	71	25	4
Line managers	75	23	2
Graduate staff	67	25	8
Technical/Specialist staff	65	31	4
Admin staff	64	32	7
Skilled manual	67	29	4
Semi-skilled/Unskilled manual	63	28	9
The respect you get from supervisors/line managers			
Aerospace	59	35	6
NHS/Loc govt	59	33	7
Finance	78	15	7
Line managers	75	21	4
Graduate staff	61	29	10
Technical/Specialist staff	63	31	6
Admin staff	67	26	7
Skilled manual	51	42	7
Semi-skilled/Unskilled manual	47	46	7
The amount of pay you receive			
Aerospace	37	59	4
NHS/Loc govt	38	60	2
Finance	41	53	4
Line managers	48	49	3
Graduate staff	50	46	4
Technical/Specialist staff	28	68	4
Admin staff	45	51	4
Skilled manual	36	61	3
Semi-skilled/Unskilled manual	28	69	3

rates at the six organisations are likely to be lower than the picture presented in Table 2.7.

The results of the multivariate analysis highlight a number of patterns (Table 2.8). First, and confirming the patterns in Table 2.7, job satisfaction was higher in the finance companies compared to aerospace and the two public sector organisations. Second, satisfaction was lower for manual workers and significantly so for the semi-/unskilled worker group. Third, the relationship between job satisfaction and

Table 2.8 Characteristics associated with job satisfaction

	Unstandardised beta coefficients	Significance
(Constant)	2.849	***
NHS/Loc govt (ref. Aero)	−0.032	
Finance	0.160	***
Line managers (ref. admin staff)	0.165	***
Graduate staff	0.040	
Technical/Specialist staff	−0.050	
Skilled manual	−0.037	
Semi-skilled manual	−0.141	**
Male (ref. female)	−0.052	
BME (ref. White British)	−0.109	
< 2 years service (ref. > 10 years)	0.106	
2–5 years service	0.028	*
5–10 years service	−0.017	
Age 16–24 years (> 50 years)	−0.060	
Age 25–29 years	−0.070	
Age 30–39 years	−0.095	**
Age 40–49 years	−0.082	**
Temporary worker (ref. permanent)	0.056	
Agency worker	0.042	
Union member (ref. non-union)	−0.056	*
Average weekly hours	−0.005	***
Increase in responsibility	0.185	***
Increase in skill	0.058	**
Increase in flexibility	−0.012	
Increase in amount of work	−0.052	***
Increase in weekly hours	−0.161	**
$R^2 = 0.099$		
N = 1912		

Note: *** = significant at 1% level ($p \leq 0.01$), ** = significant at 5% level ($p \leq 0.05$), * = significant at 10% level ($p \leq 0.10$).

age followed a u-shaped curve in that, compared to younger workers and those aged 50 and over, it was significantly lower for those in the two age groups 30–39 and 40–49. This relationship has also been found by Clark et al. (1996). Finally, there were a number of associations between satisfaction and our job recomposition and work intensity variables. Specifically, increases in job responsibilities and skill levels were associated with higher satisfaction, but patterns of intensive and extensive effort (increases in the amount of work completed each week and working hours) were linked to lower satisfaction.

Employee commitment

Like job satisfaction, employee commitment to organisational values and objectives is regarded as a core psychological facet of the HPW. It is argued that if the conditions for more favourable employee outcomes are in place, that is, HPWS conditions which generate greater employee participation, skill development and rewards at work, then workers are more likely to feel committed to their employers and more likely to offer more effective discretionary effort (Appelbaum et al., 2000; Kinnie et al., 2005).

Our survey conceptualised commitment by exploring the extent to which workers identified with their employer and accepted its goals and values (Lincoln and Kalleberg, 1990). Our commitment questions bore close similarities to the measures used by Gallie et al. (2001:1086), a scale that has been rigorously tested in USA surveys. We also adopted three questions from the WERS 1998 and 2004 surveys. Employees were asked whether they shared many of the values of their employer, whether they felt loyal to their employer, whether they were willing to work harder to help their organisation succeed and whether they would turn down another job with more pay in order to stay with their organisation. The results of these are presented in Table 2.9. Two additional questions (whether they felt proud to tell people who they worked for, and whether they would take on almost any job to keep working for their organisation) were added to create an organisational commitment scale. These six questions had an internal consistency reliability (Cronbach's alpha) of 0.7975.

Table 2.9 presents a mixed picture. On the first three indicators, worker commitment seemed to be relatively high, albeit with some differences between sectors and occupational groups. However, perhaps

Table 2.9   Indicators of organisational commitment

	Strongly agree %	Agree %	Disagree %	Strongly disagree %	Undecided %
Share many of the values of my employer					
Aerospace	6	58	19	3	14
NHS/Loc govt	4	52	23	4	18
Finance	5	61	14	2	18
Line managers	11	68	10	2	9
Graduate staff	4	60	19	4	13
Technical/Specialist staff	3	57	22	3	15
Admin staff	4	56	15	1	24
Skilled manual	5	52	26	5	12
Semi-skilled/ Unskilled manual	4	44	25	7	20
Feel loyal to my employer					
Aerospace	13	59	16	4	8
NHS/Loc govt	11	52	18	4	14
Finance	16	60	11	1	12
Line managers	22	61	9	3	5
Graduate staff	8	55	21	4	12
Technical/Specialist staff	9	60	19	3	9
Admin staff	12	58	12	3	15
Skilled manual	12	53	20	6	9
Semi-skilled/ Unskilled manual	15	47	14	6	18
Willing to work harder to help the organisation succeed					
Aerospace	12	63	14	3	8
NHS/Loc govt	9	45	28	6	12
Finance	11	55	17	3	14
Line managers	19	62	12	3	4
Graduate staff	8	56	19	5	12
Technical/Specialist staff	9	53	22	4	12
Admin staff	8	56	19	2	15
Skilled manual	11	61	17	4	7
Semi-skilled/ Unskilled manual	12	43	23	7	15
Would turn down another job with more pay in order to stay with this organisation					
Aerospace	2	13	42	22	21
NHS/Loc govt	2	12	35	35	16

(Continued)

Table 2.9   (Continued)

	Strongly agree %	Agree %	Disagree %	Strongly disagree %	Undecided %
Finance	2	11	36	28	23
Line managers	1	18	39	23	19
Graduate staff	2	11	34	32	21
Technical/Specialist staff	1	10	40	30	19
Admin staff	2	7	46	25	20
Skilled manual	3	15	40	23	19
Semi-skilled/ Unskilled manual	4	16	25	35	20

the more incisive indicator of strong organisational commitment is whether workers are prepared to forgo better paid jobs in the external labour market in order to stay with their employer. Here, the results negate the pattern of commitment provided by the other indicators: very large majorities of workers across sectors and occupations disagreed with this proposition. This result (and the job satisfaction results) suggests that despite the prevailing rhetoric governing the importance of the quality of work and associated relationships, worker attachment to these employers remained predominantly instrumental in nature.

The multivariate analysis highlights a number of additional patterns (Table 2.10). The first is an interesting sectoral result. Despite the traditions of the 'model employer' in the public sector – and the additional factors of commitment to the profession and public service – worker commitment in the local government and NHS trust establishments was significantly lower. There was also an occupational effect. Commitment was significantly lower for graduate staff and technical/specialist workers, a pattern that was partly a function of their more favourable labour market position. Another notable pattern was that younger workers and, indeed, all age groups below the age of 50 were less committed to their employers. This result, along with the results for task discretion and job satisfaction, would seem to indicate that there is little evidence in these establishments for the creation of a more satisfied and committed younger generation of workers.

Two other factors stand out. The first is that agency workers were significantly (and predictably) less committed than their colleagues

Table 2.10   Characteristics associated with employee commitment

	Unstandardised beta coefficients	Significance
(Constant)	2.861	***
NHS/Loc govt (ref. Aero)	−0.236	***
Finance	0.036	
Line managers (ref. admin staff)	0.002	
Graduate staff	−0.167	**
Technical/Specialist staff	−0.157	***
Skilled manual	−0.058	
Semi-skilled manual	−0.089	
Male (ref. female)	−0.007	
BME (ref. White British)	0.003	
<2 years service (ref. >10 years)	0.206	***
2–5 years service	0.039	
5–10 years service	−0.006	
Age 16–24 years (>50 years)	−0.166	**
Age 25–29 years	−0.151	***
Age 30–39 years	−0.185	***
Age 40–49 years	−0.097	***
Temporary worker (ref. permanent)	−0.130	
Agency worker	−0.325	***
Union member (ref. non-union)	−0.079	**
Average weekly hours	−0.001	
Increase in responsibility	0.082	**
Increase in skill	0.049	
Increase in flexibility	−0.059	
Increase in amount of work	0.008	
Increase in weekly hours	−0.009	
$R^2 = 0.089$		
N = 1902		

Note: *** = significant at 1% level (p ≤ 0.01), ** = significant at 5% level (p ≤ 0.05), * = significant at 10% level (p ≤ 0.10).

on permanent contracts. The second is that trade union members were less committed than non-union members. This could be due to a more general tendency of union members to distrust managers and become more dissatisfied with them compared with non-union members (Bryson, 2001). Citing the work of Freeman and Medoff (1984) and Gallie et al. (1998), Bryson notes that this may be due to the work values of union members who may tend to be more critical of management per se and the politicisation of unionised workers resulting in their becoming more conscious of managerial shortcomings (2001, p. 98).

Staff consultation

The concept of worker participation in decision-making processes that affect work design and broader organisational concerns is a core dimension of the HPW. Equally, advocates of the model argue that meaningful participation is impossible without equipping workers with the necessary information and knowledge required to engage with decision-making processes at multiple levels. Apart from skills training, direct employee communications and consultation techniques are held to be key supports for this. Of course, such renewed interest in direct consultation is not necessarily a function of an 'enlightened management' adopting a high-performance/high commitment approach to employee relations. In larger organisations especially, it has long been held as a means to displace union activity and influence (Forth and Millward, 2002; Metcalf, 2005; Terry, 1995).

Our opening analysis of the types of HPWS practices used by the six organisations highlighted the widespread use of a range of direct (and indirect) consultation techniques (see Table 2.1). But to what extent did these translate into meaningful consultation on issues that affect workers' pay, working conditions and employment security? To investigate this question the survey asked employees how frequently their managers asked them for their views on four themes: future plans for the workplace; staffing issues (including redundancy); changes to work practices; and pay issues. Four questions were used to derive a consultation scale (Cronbach's alpha = 0.837).

The general picture to emerge was one of decidedly limited staff consultation irrespective of sector. Majorities of respondents indicated that they were hardly ever or never consulted on these issues with very large proportions indicating this for consultation over staffing issues and pay (Table 2.11). Also noteworthy was a degree of polarisation between occupational groups, with line managers and, for some themes, non-manual workers indicating greater consultation than the two manual worker groups. The regression model confirmed this manual/non-manual divide (Table 2.12). Other patterns highlighted by the model were that consultation was lower for agency staff compared to permanent workers, lower for some groups with less

Table 2.11   Employees' assessment of the extent of direct consultation, by sector and occupational class

Occupational group	Frequently %	Sometimes %	Hardly ever %	Never %
How often do managers ask you for your views on future plans for the workplace				
Aerospace	9	33	32	26
NHS/Loc govt	9	33	30	28
Finance	9	39	32	20
Line managers	24	40	26	10
Graduate staff	11	40	32	17
Technical/Specialist staff	8	36	33	23
Admin staff	6	34	32	28
Skilled manual	3	28	34	35
Semi-skilled/ Unskilled manual	3	25	29	43
How often do managers ask you for your views on staffing issues, including redundancies				
Aerospace	6	18	30	46
NHS/Loc govt	6	21	30	43
Finance	5	22	36	37
Line managers	19	32	25	24
Graduate staff	6	18	40	36
Technical/Specialist staff	4	22	32	42
Admin staff	4	16	31	49
Skilled manual	2	12	30	56
Semi-skilled/ Unskilled manual	1	11	28	60
How often do managers ask you for your views on changes to work practices				
Aerospace	9	40	30	21
NHS/Loc govt	10	37	27	26
Finance	14	46	25	15
Line managers	24	43	25	8
Graduate staff	10	45	29	16
Technical/Specialist staff	11	43	26	20
Admin staff	9	40	25	26
Skilled manual	4	37	34	25
Semi-skilled/ Unskilled manual	4	28	31	37
How often do managers ask you for your views on pay issues				
Aerospace	2	14	31	52
NHS/Loc govt	3	14	29	55
Finance	5	21	41	34
Line managers	9	23	36	32

(Continued)

Table 2.11   (Continued)

Occupational group	Frequently %	Sometimes %	Hardly ever %	Never %
Graduate staff	3	12	36	49
Technical/Specialist staff	2	15	32	51
Admin staff	1	15	28	56
Skilled manual	1	12	28	59
Semi-skilled/ Unskilled manual	2	11	27	60

Table 2.12   Characteristics associated with consultation

	Unstandardised beta coefficients	Significance
(Constant)	1.815	***
NHS/Loc govt (ref. Aero)	0.056	
Finance	−0.009	
Line managers (ref. admin staff)	0.515	***
Graduate staff	0.148	**
Technical/Specialist staff	0.111	**
Skilled manual	−0.097	*
Semi-skilled manual	−0.220	***
Male (ref. female)	0.042	
BME (ref. White British)	−0.011	
< 2 years service (ref. > 10 years)	0.053	
2–5 years service	−0.111	***
5–10 years service	−0.089	*
Age 16–24 years (> 50 years)	−0.004	
Age 25–29 years	0.074	
Age 30–39 years	−0.017	
Age 40–49 years	−0.002	
Temporary worker (ref. permanent)	−0.108	
Agency worker	−0.479	***
Union member (ref. non-union)	−0.025	
Average weekly hours	0.001	
Increase in responsibility	0.159	***
Increase in skill	0.028	
Increase in flexibility	−0.140	
Increase in amount of work	0.120	
Increase in weekly hours	0.094	*
$R^2 = 0.140$		
$N = 2229$		

Note: *** = significant at 1% level ($p \leq 0.01$), ** = significant at 5% level ($p \leq 0.05$), * = significant at 10% level ($p \leq 0.10$).

employment service and higher for those workers reporting increases in job responsibilities.

This pattern corresponded with the more representative WERS 1998 survey results (the last time this question was used). They confirm that direct consultation is a much weaker – and ineffective – form of 'employee voice' compared to union representation and one that seems unsustainable as a means of substituting union communications.

Workplace stress

Perhaps one of the more controversial facets of Appelbaum et al.'s (2000) thesis is that one of the by-products of high-performance work practices is lower levels of workplace stress. This is potentially contentious in the light of many analyses of contemporary experiences of work in the industrialised economies that suggest workplace stress is on the increase (Chandler et al., 2003; CIPD, 2006a; Cooper et al., 2001; TUC, 2006). For Appelbaum et al., the distinctive feature of quality of working life in the HPW model is that when workers are provided opportunities to participate in decision-making processes then commitment and satisfaction will increase while work-related stress will decrease. The assumption is that employee participation will be founded on higher trust relationships and more rewarding jobs (2000: 167–8).

Our data did not entirely support this confident assertion. Employees were asked whether or not they agreed with four statements governing job security, having enough time to complete tasks, worrying a lot about their work outside working hours, and feeling very tired at the end of the work day. The last three of these were used to derive a workplace stress scale (Cronbach's alpha = 0.684).

The results showed that considerable proportions of workers experienced these types of job-related stressors, albeit with significant variation across sectors and occupations (Table 2.13). For example, job security was relatively high in the public sector and finance establishments but much lower in the aerospace plants. It was also much lower for skilled manual workers compared to other groups. The experience of never having enough time to get jobs completed was fairly common across occupational groups and relatively high in the public sector establishments. Worrying a lot about work outside working hours was an experience reported by a surprisingly large minority of workers, particularly in the public sector establishments and for supervisory

Table 2.13 Workplace stress patterns, by sector and occupational class

	Strongly agree %	Agree %	Disagree %	Strongly disagree %	Undecided %
I feel my job is secure in this workplace					
Aerospace	4	36	36	14	10
NHS/Loc govt	20	53	15	5	7
Finance	11	53	17	7	12
Line managers	9	48	26	6	11
Graduate staff	14	53	19	6	8
Technical/Specialist staff	14	49	22	8	7
Admin staff	7	47	22	8	16
Skilled manual	3	27	42	19	9
Semi-skilled/ Unskilled manual	17	47	20	10	6
I never seem to have enough time to get my job done					
Aerospace	12	35	44	3	5
NHS/Loc govt	21	36	35	3	5
Finance	14	32	42	7	5
Line managers	21	47	28	1	3
Graduate staff	24	31	38	5	3
Technical/Specialist staff	19	39	36	2	4
Admin staff	11	32	44	5	7
Skilled manual	7	27	56	5	5
Semi-skilled/ Unskilled manual	17	33	36	4	10
I worry a lot about my work outside working hours					
Aerospace	5	23	48	20	4
NHS/Loc govt	10	24	44	18	4
Finance	4	21	44	25	6
Line managers	12	30	44	9	5
Graduate staff	7	25	44	20	4
Technical/Specialist staff	6	27	48	16	3
Admin staff	5	21	49	22	3
Skilled manual	4	17	45	29	4
Semi-skilled/ Unskilled manual	7	17	45	24	7
I feel very tired at the end of a work day					
Aerospace	13	49	30	3	5
NHS/Loc govt	30	48	16	2	4

(Continued)

Table 2.13   (Continued)

	Strongly agree %	Agree %	Disagree %	Strongly disagree %	Undecided %
Finance	14	46	30	3	7
Line managers	20	53	24	1	2
Graduate staff	18	45	27	4	7
Technical/Specialist staff	19	49	25	1	5
Admin staff	14	48	28	3	7
Skilled manual	14	50	27	4	5
Semi-skilled/ Unskilled manual	36	38	18	3	5

and non-manual workers. Large majorities of workers in all occupational groups and sectors reported feeling very tired at the end of the work day and particularly workers in the public sector establishments, line managers and semi-/unskilled workers.

Table 2.14 presents the results for sectoral and worker characteristics associated with the workplace stress scale. These confirm that workplace stress was higher in the public sector establishments. There was an occupational effect in that stress was higher for line managers and white-collar technical/specialist staff compared to the administrative staff reference group. The model also shows a significant association between gender and workplace stress in that stress was higher for the female reference group. Apart from job-related stressors that are compounded by manifestations of gender inequality in the private sphere, this result is also attributable to the relatively large proportion of women workers in the public sector establishments. Trade union membership was another factor that was found to be positively associated with stress. Accounting for this is not straightforward in the six organisations under study, but it might be partly related to tendencies for union members to distrust managers and to voice dissatisfaction based on their greater awareness of workplace problems (Freeman and Medoff, 1984).

The different job recomposition and labour intensification variables provided a more robust set of positive associations with stress. Increases in job responsibilities and in the amount of work that workers were expected to complete each week were both positively associated – and both factors were reported by large numbers of workers in these high-performance management regimes (see Table 2.3). Both longer weekly

Table 2.14 Characteristics associated with workplace stress

	Unstandardised Beta Coefficients	Significance
(Constant)	1.971	***
NHS/Loc Govt (ref. Aero)	0.192	***
Finance	−0.016	
Line managers (ref. admin staff)	0.175	***
Graduate staff	0.025	
Technical/Specialist staff	0.136	***
Skilled manual	−0.083	*
Semi-skilled manual	0.080	
Male (ref. female)	−0.095	**
BME (ref. White British)	0.012	
< 2 years service (ref. > 10 years)	−0.051	
2–5 years service	−0.101	
5–10 years service	−0.056	***
Age 16–24 years (> 50 years)	−0.156	**
Age 25–29 years	−0.029	
Age 30–39 years	0.019	
Age 40–49 years	0.022	
Temporary worker (ref. permanent)	−0.071	
Agency worker	−0.190	*
Union member (ref. non-union)	0.062	**
Average weekly hours	0.007	***
Increase in responsibility	0.123	***
Increase in skill	−0.006	
Increase in flexibility	0.013	
Increase in amount of work	0.264	***
Increase in weekly hours	0.217	***
$R^2 = 0.237$		
N = 1943		

Note: *** = significant at 1% level ($p \leq 0.01$), ** = significant at 5% level ($p \leq 0.05$), * = significant at 10% level ($p \leq 0.10$).

hours and increases in weekly hours were also positively associated with stress. Overall, these results hardly paint a picture of lower job-related stress levels in high-performance work regimes; if anything, the opposite is true.

Union performance

The themes of trade union relations and organising forms are important for HPW debates. While union recognition is not regarded as essential, many HPW advocates argue that the existence of influential but cooperative workplace unions can help generate greater social cohesion at work and thus bolster the legitimacy of management reforms. For example, in a recent edited collection on the subject different writers noted that the HPW model contains a number of contradictions for workers. Not the least of these are the coexistence of productive flexibility and process standardisation, and the tensions between the principles of knowledge-work, self-regulation and multi-skilling and the organisational context of organising cooperation and increased labour productivity in a hierarchical command structure (J. Bélanger et al., 2002, p. 57). In these conditions, rather than relying on a defensive, oppositionalist stance, it is argued that workplace unions can renew themselves by adopting an autonomous, proactive position that involves a form of cooperative participation in strategic management. This also means exchanging the traditions of rank and file militancy and job control for the acquisition of new partnership rights (P. R. Bélanger et al., 2002).

Analysis of the role and efficacy of workplace partnership is, of course, a central theme of this book and one that weaves its way through each of the following case study chapters. For contextual purposes, we complete this chapter by presenting analysis of a number of survey questions that investigated the performance and influence of union activity in five out of the six establishments (this excluded the non-union FinanceCo). Trade union members were asked two questions governing union performance directly in relation to the members themselves (taking notice of member problems and union communications) and four questions governing union influence at work (being taken seriously by management, making a difference at work, influence over pay and influence over working conditions). A union performance scale was derived from these six questions (Cronbach's Alpha = 0.824).

Since analysis of occupational difference showed no clear distinction between groups, only sectoral differences are presented (Table 2.15). The first two questions concerned servicing membership problems and communications. In both cases union performance was higher in the aerospace establishments (a sector where rank and file union organisation has been traditionally robust and militant) and lower in the two public sector establishments (where decentralised rank and file activity is a relatively new development). Union influence over

Table 2.15 Trade union members' assessment of union influence and perform-ance, by sector

	Strongly agree %	Agree %	Disagree %	Strongly disagree %	Undecided %
Unions here take notice of members' problems and complaints					
Aerospace	13	71	8	2	6
NHS/Loc govt	8	50	15	3	24
InsuranceCo	19	61	0	2	9
Unions here are good at communicating with members					
Aerospace	8	56	24	4	8
NHS/Loc govt	3	35	30	6	25
InsuranceCo	11	44	20	4	20
Unions here are taken seriously by management					
Aerospace	3	50	32	5	10
NHS/Loc govt	4	40	21	3	31
InsuranceCo	11	67	4	2	17
Unions here make a difference to what it is like to work here					
Aerospace	9	66	14	2	9
NHS/Loc govt	3	35	27	3	33
InsuranceCo	13	33	19	4	32
Unions here have a lot of influence over pay					
Aerospace	5	33	44	7	11
NHS/Loc govt	2	22	36	10	29
InsuranceCo	7	21	38	8	26
Unions here have a lot of influence over working conditions					
Aerospace	6	61	23	2	9
NHS/Loc govt	2	34	29	6	29
InsuranceCo	11	35	30	4	20

management, pay and conditions was also higher in the aerospace establishments (based on three out of the four indicators). One other notable factor was that most members felt that their unions did not exert a lot of influence over pay, a reflection perhaps of the negative impact of low inflation on a core union activity (and for the public sector workers, the constraints of central government budgetary policy).

The negative association between the public sector establishments and union performance is confirmed in the model presented in Table 2.16. This also highlights a u-shaped relationship between the age of workers and their assessment of union performance (the youngest and oldest age groups rate union performance higher than those aged between 25 and 49 years). As we saw in Table 2.8, the same relationship existed between age and job satisfaction. This suggests a potential (and partial) line of causation between satisfaction with the union and broader job satisfaction at work (although the direction of causation is open to question). Finally, and notably, the model shows that working in a partnership environment was negatively associated with union performance. The meaning and implication of

Table 2.16 Characteristics associated with union performance (union members only)

	Unstandardised beta coefficients	Significance
(Constant)	2.959	***
NHS/Loc govt (ref. Aero)	−0.237	***
InsuranceCo	0.257	*
Partnership (ref. non-partnership)	−0.112	***
Line managers (ref. admin staff)	0.039	
Graduate staff	0.180	
Technical/Specialist staff	0.042	
Skilled manual	−0.002	
Semi-skilled Manual	−0.155	*
Male (ref. female)	0.046	
BME (ref. White British)	0.062	
<2 years service (ref. >10 years)	0.200	**
2–5 years service	−0.020	
5–10 years service	−0.057	
Age 16–24 years (>50 years)	0.140	*
Age 25–29 years	−0.122	**
Age 30–39 years	−0.112	***
Age 40–49 years	−0.086	**
Temporary worker (ref. permanent)	−0.251	
Agency worker	−0.393	
Average weekly hours	−0.004	
Increase in responsibility	−0.011	
Increase in skill	−0.011	
Increase in flexibility	−0.004	
Increase in amount of work	0.019	
Increase in weekly hours	0.072	*
$R^2 = 0.075$		
N = 1308		

Note: *** = significant at 1% level (p ≤ 0.01), ** = significant at 5% level (p ≤ 0.05), * = significant at 10% level (p ≤ 0.10).

this result is covered in all its complexity in the following chapters of this book.

Conclusion

We have provided some evidence of positive worker outcomes in the case study establishments, each of which had adopted a good quantity of high-performance work practices over the years, leading up to the research. For example, a recasting of jobs and tasks had clearly taken shape with many workers reporting increases in skills and responsibilities and increases in the degree of flexibility required in their work. This was accompanied by relatively high task discretion for some. Apart from the question of remuneration, job satisfaction also seemed high with a good number of workers reporting satisfaction with such themes as job influence, sense of achievement at work and supervisory relations. Equally, there was some evidence that worker commitment was high, although the thorny question of commitment to what exactly was more debatable. For example, the fact that so many workers disagreed with the idea that they would turn down a better paying job with an alternative employer in order to stay with the current one seemed to suggest that their commitment was more 'instrumental' and one based on deeper questions of economic dependency in neoliberal capitalist society.

On the other hand, we have also raised a series of contradictions, unequal outcomes and, more generally, negative outcomes for these workers. For example, many of the positive patterns summarised above applied much less so to skilled manual workers and especially semi-skilled and unskilled workers. To some degree, the same can be said for the minority of agency workers employed in some of the six organisations.

The recasting of jobs and job roles alongside, as we shall see, organisational restructuring, labour rationalisation and sheer competitive pressure, has also led to clear evidence of increases in workers' intensive and extensive effort. The upshot of this has been a widespread experience of different job stressors and workplace stress. At the same time, the survey results do not support the hypothesis that these 'high performance tensions' can be lessened by any managerial attempts to engender social cohesion through more cooperative employment relations. One manifestation of this might have been the provision of greater direct 'employee voice' through more meaningful staff consultation. Another would be the provision of greater indirect employee voice by offering trade unions greater influence over organisational decision-making processes under the auspices of workplace partnership arrangements. Despite the fact that direct and indirect consultation techniques were well embedded at each of the case study establishments, and despite the existence of workplace partnership in some of these, our data showed that worker outcomes were mostly negative. Management's performance in directly consulting workers was seen to be predominantly weak, and worse still for manual workers and agency staff. And evaluation of union performance declined for workers located in partnership environments compared to those based in work areas where management–union relations were more conventionally adversarial.

By presenting these rudimentary patterns we have attempted to provide some initial insights into the nature of worker outcomes in the six high-performance work organisations under study. As such we have established parameters for the more qualitative case study chapters that address the question of why things appear as they do along with the complexity of local variations in capitalist workplace dynamics. Perhaps the key point of departure for this is that our survey data analysis suggests that the HPW model, situated as it is in a neoliberal managerial rhetoric, does not – and cannot – deliver on its ostensible 'win-win' agenda. The four private sector establishments in this study, like any other large UK firm, operated in highly competitive markets, which required them to maximise profitability and shareholder value. The two public sector organisations operated in a parallel world of marketisation and strict budgetary control. These broader economic environments generated exploitative labour process conditions and different forms of labour control in a conflictual capitalist employment relationship. As we shall see, it is no surprise, therefore, if workers come to view the management reforms of the HPW – and workplace partnership – as problematic, contradictory and contestable.

3
Gambling with Employee Voice in the Finance Sector

The finance sector

The finance sector in the UK now employs one in five of the workforce (Labour Force Survey, 2006). As such it is an important sector to study. Rapid growth in the sector followed the 1980s 'revolution' in the regulatory regime governing the provision of financial services (Moran, 1991), with employment in 'banking, finance and insurance' growing from just under 3 million in 1980 to 4.5 million in 1990, and then to 5.5 million in 2000 (www.statistics.gov.uk). The new regime opened up competition in the sector leading to fierce struggles for market share and the blurring of traditional divides between 'product' suppliers both at home and abroad. The period of post-war corporate relative stability gave way to a spate of mergers and new alliances, encouraging both capital concentration within the sector and the emergence of new specialist market entrants based first on the telephone (such as *Direct Line*), and then on the internet and alternative spatial outlets such as the supermarket. Banks began to sell insurance and give mortgages, while building societies began to offer current accounts. De/re-regulation and demutualisation were reasons for the emergence of a new management 'model' whereby the old model based on paternalism, conservatism and bureaucracy gave way to a model of sales and performance orientation and technocracy (Cressey and Scott, 1992). As such, the old certainties of work and organisational hierarchy began to crumble, and new technology was fully utilised in the process. Morris et al. (2001), record that to begin with 'technological advances were benign in the sense that they allowed business expansion with productivity and employment growth'. However, recession hit the national economy in the early 1990s and this provoked a period of cost containment in the sector engendering de-layering within organisations, combined with internal business restructuring and even more mergers and acquisitions. Thus while employment totals in the sector continued to increase in total, individual organisations were being restructured and affected by job loss and job restructure. Employer efforts to enhance individual employee productivity and value added also acted as a spur for major upheavals in the organisation of work. As a result employees have been faced not only with job insecurity but also with constant revisions to job titles and skill requirements. The challenges for human resource management and employee relations have been immense. In particular, the move towards a sales and entrepreneurial focus entailed a process of attitudinal restructuring of employees. This has involved the abandonment of incremental grade pay and the injection of alternative pay frameworks which downgraded the negotiating role of employee representatives. Individual performance-related pay is now dominant within the sector, supplemented in many instances with competency-based pay, team bonuses and market-related supplements. Work has been intensified through the establishment of task-based teams, business process re-engineering, the establishment of semi-autonomous business divisions and the injection of computer-based work procedures. A division of skills has also occurred between mainly routinised jobs tied to computer-based inputs, and 'knowledge-based' jobs tied to computer-based outputs (Danford et al., 2003, pp. 97–121). Within this polarisation of skills many jobs have been reformulated in call centres, based either in the UK or outsourced abroad (Bain and Taylor, 2003).

This shift in organisation culture and ownership in the sector has been accompanied with a major change in employee relations' regimes. Historically, there has been significant presence of dependent and independent staff association as well as some trade union representation within the sector. In general terms, the sector can thus be characterised by its mix of employee representation and employee voice regimes. The relatively high presence of staff associations is a product of the former authoritarian paternalistic employee relations culture which was integral to the development of financial institutions. Employer paternalism was the enabling mechanism whereby employee relations were kept 'in-house' often, at least in building societies, in fairly small establishments rooted in region or town. Employers allowed some voice within the organisation but kept their employees away from the 'vulgarities' of the TUC and its affiliates. Until the financial services revolution, jobs were relatively secure with defined career structures (at least for males), work organisation was stable, and pay and benefits better than average. Employers were thus able to hold the line against independent unionism simply because employees were unconvinced of the need for adversarialism and the concomitant 'dual loyalty' required by trade union membership. Within the banking industry the National Union of Bank Employees (NUBE) had nevertheless sought to undermine the staff associations since the 1940s, achieving some success in persuading staff associations to transfer. The remaining staff associations grew in size throughout the 1970s, reflecting the general collectivisation of white-collar workers in that decade. However, in the building societies and insurance companies the employers, no doubt acting collectively, managed to hold out longer against union insurgence, and the predominance of staff associations persisted. Despite this the National Union of Insurance Workers recorded some success in creating independent unionism, while the first Guild of Insurance Officials (GIO) renamed itself to the Union of Insurance Staffs (UIS) before transferring to ASTMS in 1970.

The introduction of human resource policies driven by market competition from the 1980s onwards meant that the 'old' employee relations' regimes were challenged. In the banking industry an upturn in union combativeness expressed in industrial disputes gathered pace during the 1990s, culminating at its peak in 1997 (Gall, 1999, 2001a). Gall (2001a, p. 359) records that 'strike action began to become an acceptable currency among union members and a more "normal" part of the industrial relations landscape within banking'. This is not to suggest that the finance sector became a central focus of militancy. Strike activity where it did take place was largely confined to the banks rather than building societies and insurance companies. However, it can be said that industrial relations in the sector matured in the period. Explanation for this increased union combativeness lies in the perceived need of employees to defend their position within the rapidly changing work environment. Storey et al. (1998, p. 16), for example, refer to a general deterioration of industrial relations in the banking industry due to 'accumulated grievances' and a 'low ebb' of staff trust in management. Snape et al. (1993), in referring to building societies, found that employees 'were expressing a demand for stronger collective representation as a protection against uncertainty'. The cost containment strategies pursued by the employers are argued by Gall (1999) to have been the cause of the corresponding rise in the 'unionateness' of the unions in the sector. Indeed, union density across the sector rose to a peak of 54 per cent in 1994 before falling back in the latter part of the 1990s (Waddington, 2001), and both unions and staff associations were expressing a willingness to confront the employer more so than before. The unions also appeared to forego their earlier hostility to staff associations and began to tempt those in existence into alliances and mergers. The key unions established the Alliance for Finance in 1996 and, in doing so, they embraced many of the staff associations in discussions and talks in the atmosphere of a 'dating agency' (Radcliffe, 1997). What followed was a parallel concentration of forces as the staff associations drifted towards the independent unions. It was this alliance that paved the way for the creation of UNIFI in 1999, by combining the Bank, Insurance and Finance Union – BIFU (formerly NUBE), the Nat West Staff Association and UNiFI. The National Union of Insurance Workers developed an accommodation with the MSF (formerly ASTMS) before merging fully in 2000. MSF then merged with the engineers' union to form Amicus. In 2004, UNIFI transferred its 150,000 members to Amicus, which then became the dominant finance sector union in the UK with a combined total of over 200,000 members in the sector. In 2007, the old Amicus section of the newly created UNITE claimed some form of representation in 23 building societies and at least ten major insurance companies (www.amicus.org.uk). A further eight building society 'stand-alone' staff associations were directly affiliated to the TUC. Many more staff associations within the industry are registered as independent unions with the Certification Office but remain outside of the TUC (see Figure 3.1).

The cocktail of rapidly changing human resource practices and employee drift towards collectivism and adversarialism created a dilemma for the employers. How could the employers manage the process of change within organisations and at the same time contain bubbling dissent from disaffected employees in a tightening labour market? This dilemma was framed within the desire of the employers to move towards a high productivity, high-commitment model of management in order to survive competitively. Such a resource-based model could be interpreted as a 'one best way' to utilise the creativity

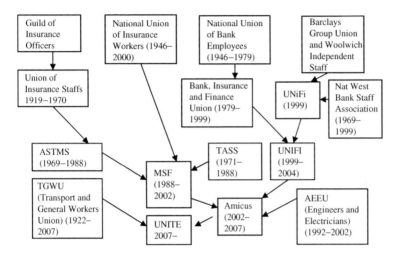

Figure 3.1   The recent consolidation of TUC affiliate unions in the finance sector.
Note: For complete historical chart see www.unionancestors.co.uk

of the workforce in a restructured working environment where employers were keen to develop value added from its employees. As we have already outlined in our introductory chapter the HPWS route would also mean a commitment to creating vehicles for employee voice within a 'partnership' framework. In an industrial sector awash with a multichannel employee representation, the prospect of 'fitting-in' with the European Works Council directive and the 2004 Information and Consultation of Employees Regulations was an added spur to reformulate employee relations strategy towards enhanced consultation. Utilising Fox's (1974) typologies of management style we can discern that many employers adapted to the new employee combativeness and the more pluralist framework by consolidating a 'sophisticated modern' approach, while at the same time diluting aspects of the former authoritarian paternalism. To secure a sustainable partnership route, certain risks had to be faced by employers. To cite Freeman and Medoff (1984, p. 108), in order to utilise employee voice 'management [must] give up power and accept a dual authority channel ... [but] if management gives up power it creates the genuine seeds of unions; if it doesn't, employee representation plans may be mere window dressing'. We can trace these employer strategies and dilemma in both the unionised and non-unionised sections of the sector.

The unionised section

If the employers wished to travel down the partnership route, then wherever unions had a presence they would have to be brought on board the ship. For many employers in the sector, authoritarian paternalism still formed the backdrop of their employee relations strategy. The infusion of more open Human Resource Management (HRM) practices of employee involvement might be difficult to implement or sustain due to collective or individual management intransigence. This was certainly found to be the case in the majority of insurance companies surveyed by Danford et al. (2003), where continued management hostility to the expression of employee voice was to the fore. A move towards a partnership agenda, allowing the legitimation of employee voice and representation, would therefore mean a revision of the employer-union relationship. *Both* sides of the industrial divide would have to forego adversarialism for consensus and cooperation to work. From the late 1990s we can indeed detect evidence of an emerging partnership agenda within the sector wherein the unions were complicit with management. Gall (2001a) detects a surge of employer generated partnership agreements signed in the sector from 1997 onwards, which embraced MSF, BIFU, NUIW, UNiFI and UNIFI, as well as the NatWest Staff Association, the Lloyds Trade Union and the AXA and Britannia Building Society staff associations. Gall (ibid., p. 365) further suggests that union agreement to partnership underlined 'the limits of new-found collective strength' whereby the unions 'are not in a position to reject the partnership agreements wholesale and impose an alternative type of arrangement based on quite different principles'. Such a view is supported by Wills's (2004) study of the new partnership agreement at Barclays signed with UNiFi in 1998. A breakdown in relationships between the management and unions in the strike of 1997 was then followed by major staff reductions. Wills claims that the union agreed to partnership in Barclays as a way of resecuring legitimacy and representation. This is not to suggest that the union embrace of partnership has been undertaken without dissent from sections of union activists within the sector. Samuel (2005), in his research on partnership between Amicus and Legal and General, found important tensions arising between union activists and union leadership over the agreement. The tension was eventually smoothed only by the creation of management-supported cadre of 'cultivated' pro-partnership union activists drawn from the junior and professional staff in the organisation. Gall (2001a) also records minority union dissent to partnership both within Barclays and the Co-Operative banks.

The non-union environment

Outside of the unionised sections of the sector, the pressures for change stemming from EU policy, government and employer interest in partnership are equally apparent. In particular, forms of non-union employee representation are becoming increasingly evident in the UK as the industrial relations backdrop moves towards multichannel employee representation (Gospel and Willman, 2003; Ackers et al., 2005). This commitment of government and employers to the multichannel model poses important questions that need testing by case study evidence. Public policy formerly relied on employee representation via the 'single channel' of trade unions voluntarily recognised by employers. Non-union employee representation (NER) was considered anomalous and its incidence was limited. It was most common in industries with structural characteristics associated with unionisation and consequently was assumed to be largely cosmetic, the employer's principal objective being union avoidance. The changed institutional industrial relations landscape, however, has generated a more differentiated set of views. In the light of such changing terrain there has been an emerging body of literature examining non-union workplaces, usually from within perspectives that focus on particular aspects of managerial strategy (see Dundon and Rollinson, 2004 for a review). Most studies have continued to present models describing strategies for union avoidance and the maintenance of managerial authority (Roy, 1980; Guest and Hoque, 1994; McLoughlin and Gourlay, 1994) while others have focused on product markets as contextual driving factors (Rubery, 1988; Kochan et al., 1986). Dundon and Rollinson (2004, p. 12) adapt from previous typologies created by Roy (1980) and Gall (2001b) and produce seven different non-union employer types of behaviour and practice. Some behaviours, such as 'Fear Stuff' or 'Evil Stuff', are clearly belligerent towards unions, while others, such as 'Awkward Stuff' or 'Sweet Stuff' are more pragmatic responses to possible union incursion. However, given the new institutional environment, it is now of increasing interest to examine the voice effectiveness of non-union *forms of employee representation* rather than that of non-unionism *per se*, particularly in cases where there is an expressed management preference for a partnership route to organisational effectiveness and efficiency.

As Gollan (2005) notes, debates in this field of inquiry focus on the ability of NER to match or exceed the effectiveness of trade unions as conduits of employee voice and interest. Is it the case that employees might work successfully within consultative-based mechanisms to further their interest (Bryson, 2000), or is NER a cosmetic process of employee representation that is likely to be dominated by management sympathisers (Kelly, 1996; Terry, 1999, 2003; Wills, 2000)? A sceptical view is that non-union works councils and like arrangements can provide an effective substitute for trade unions in voluntarist and decentralised industrial relations regimes such as the UK's (Hall and Terry, 2004). But NER lacks 'legally provided tools of bargaining power' (Kim and Kim, 2004, p. 1078) and is 'enterprise confined'. Without industrial action 'immunities' it cannot make credible threats of sanctions in support of employee demands, or even to hold management to its commitments to consult. Because non-union employee representatives have not had legal protection from employer's victimisation they have been inclined towards caution. The provisions of the ICE Regulations may modify some of the limitations. But the conclusion is that effective employee representation in organisation-based consultation arrangements requires the support of strong trade unions that can provide 'expertise, co-ordination and mobilising potential' (Terry, 1999, p. 29). The issue, therefore, is whether or not trade unions can insert themselves into the workplace where NER is present. NER, in this perspective, would always raise the spectre of unionisation even where management had deliberated against it.

To date, few studies have systematically compared employees' experiences of NER with union members' evaluation of their union representation. However, statistical analyses of the 1998 Workplace Employment Relations Survey (WERS98) data assess the effectiveness of different types of 'employee voice regime' in terms of employees' positive perceptions of *managerial responsiveness*; their proclivity for information sharing, employee consultation and the 'fair treatment' of employees. Bryson's (2004) analysis finds that non-union representative voice and 'direct voice' ('two way' management, direct employee communications) outperform union voice, in the terms considered. It also finds that the combination of NER and direct voice – identified in a mere 8 per cent of British workplaces in 1998 – is the only regime to outperform that of no employee voice (ibid., p. 235). The findings raise almost as many questions as the analysis set out to probe, as

Bryson is the first to admit. Explanations for the apparent ineffectiveness of union voice have been suggested in terms of unions' success in mobilising members – raising their consciousness – so that they are more critical of management practices than non-union employees (Guest and Conway, 2004). Of course, union members may also be more exacting in their expectations of their representatives, and management may be active in counter-mobilising against union power and influence. Union leaders may also be complicit in deflecting activist mobilisation by processes of collaboration with the employer (Bain and Taylor, 2001). Other analyses suggest how NER may be part of a 'bundle' of HRM practices combined to intensify management control (Hall and Terry, 2004, p. 216); that is to say the aim is to structure employee attitudes and inculcate a 'consensus culture' based on the acceptance of management objectives.

NER has also been compared with unions 'in general'. An argument is that strong trade unions are better equipped than weak and compliant unions or NER to 'coerce' management along the partnership 'high road' (Haynes and Allen, 2001). The coercion in this case is from employers who, Ackers et al. (2005) argue, are reconstructing representative employee participation with or without union involvement in order to achieve their organisational efficiency objectives, or simply to accommodate new labour law. How, then, might these particular aspects of NER be played out within the finance sector, with its own specific tradition of dependent and independent staff associations?

Summary

To summarise, it would appear that many employers in the sector have attempted to solve their employee relations dilemma by utilising the partnership framework. But while employers may have some strategic choice in determining any new employee relations regime which includes employee voice and individual commitment as key features, the *structures* and *processes* associated with such a regime may vary. In terms of chosen employer strategy there will be elements of both path dependency and path shaping in which process interplays with structure. The question arises as to how far might lingering paternalism contain employer willingness to concede employee voice? How also might unions react to an employer-driven attempt to instil processes of consultation and consensus over hard-won rights of negotiation? Further, how might employers attempt to manage partnership in a non-union environment without conceding demands for unions?

These questions frame our analysis in this chapter. Two organisations are examined. One (*FinanceCo*) is a non-union example of partnership working in an organisation which had a long history as a UK-based building society and is now owned by a British Isles based bank. The other is a German-owned insurance company (*InsuranceCo*) with trade union recognition, but where employee relations is moving towards partnership working set against the background of declining union representation. At the end of the 1990s the union accepted a collaborative relationship, that is an informal partnership arrangement with the employer. Our two case study organisations thus provide a fascinating comparison of a non-union employee relations strategy with that of a traditionally unionised one. In each case there have been pressures for change. In the former case the effectiveness of employee voice has been challenged from below, whereby in the second case it has been challenged from above. We test the effectiveness of employee voice representative mechanisms in the two organisations by focussing on the merits and demerits of the Partners' Council in FinanceCo and of the traditional negotiative arrangements in InsuranceCo. The analysis is based on more than 80 interviews across the two organisations and a wider survey of more than 250 staff.

Employee relations strategies

Our two case study organisations exhibit similarities and differences in corporate governance and product orientation. FinanceCo has experienced considerable change in ownership over the last decade, moving from a regional-based building society to a section of a multinational based with a home base outside the UK. While it continued to offer mortgage provision from local offices it had also become a more general financial service provider in its HQ building as the UK arm of the multinational. InsuranceCo, in contrast, has experienced relative corporate stability as the UK office of a German-based insurance organisation. InsuranceCo has a specialist product market with most professional and legal work undertaken in its head office and some claims work undertaken in a sub-office in a small town in the Welsh valleys. Both of the head offices of the organisations were based across the road from each other in a major city in south-west England, and so they sought staff from within the same local labour market. Both organisations had enacted substantial new working arrangements in recent years including teamworking, job rotation, performance appraisals, merit and bonus pay. While FinanceCo has never recognised trade unions, it has a consultative forum for all staff (the Partners' Council). InsuranceCo has a recognition agreement with (the then) Amicus, but has recently agreed on a partnership arrangement with the union.

Employer efforts to reorganise work can be seen clearly from Tables 3.1 and 3.2, where we ask employees how their work has changed in recent years. Employees perceive that the skills necessary to undertake their jobs have increased, together with feelings of work intensification. This might be expected, given the rapidly changing work organisation already described in the sector as a whole. Only small percentages of staff in both organisations record a decrease in expected skills, responsibilities and flexibility requirements. In InsuranceCo, however, opinion is more divided over increases in flexibility. More detailed analysis of the data for InsuranceCo suggests that this may be due to the preponderance of graduate professional grades in the organisation (lawyers, solicitors etc.) undertaking rule-bound tasks. Fifty-seven per cent report no change in levels of flexibility required, and 62 per cent report no change in levels of responsibility. Slightly

Table 3.1 Employees' assessment of changes in skill level in recent years, all respondents

	Increased (%)	Decreased (%)	Unchanged (%)
Change in the skill level required for my job			
FinanceCo	78	3	19
InsuranceCo	73	4	23
Change in the responsibility involved in my job			
FinanceCo	65	8	27
InsuranceCo	73	5	22
Change in the degree of flexibility required in my work			
FinanceCo	70	3	27
InsuranceCo	56	5	39

Note: FinanceCo, n = 128; InsuranceCo, n = 127.

Table 3.2   Employees' experience of work intensification, all respondents

	Increased (%)	Decreased (%)	Unchanged (%)
Change to the amount of work I am expected to complete each week			
FinanceCo	59	5	36
InsuranceCo	64	4	32
Change to the number of hours I am expected to work each week			
FinanceCo	14	7	79
InsuranceCo	20	3	77

Note: FinanceCo, n = 128; InsuranceCo, n = 127.

less than two-thirds of staff in both organisations have experienced an intensification of their work; however, the vast majority of staff do not report an increase in expected working hours, indicating that work intensification is a result of the reorganisation of work.

More detailed description of the work and employment relations' regimes in the organisations is now presented.

FinanceCo

Under new ownership from the late 1990s, the corporate structure was divisionalised to make managers accountable for the profit or loss performance of separate business units. The product market strategy of 'customer relationship management' was accompanied by a drive for efficiency savings from work reorganisation, including the extension of call centre operations and generic work teams. HRM practices included 'market driven' and 'merit based' pay under the rubric of a scheme entitled *Sharing in Success*. Employment totalled 2700 in 2002–3. A majority of staff worked in the consumer sales and service business unit (including the branch network), 800 were in the mortgage lending and processing business, and 300 in head office support.

The organisation had always been non-union and before the 1990s had no provision for employee representation. An enlarged HR department, however, instituted the 'partners council' (PC) system from the early 1990s as a 'management alternative to trade unions' (manager interview). All employees (including managerial staff) were automatically PC members. Workplace constituencies of 30 to 35 employees elected (by individual ballot) a representative to a PC – there was a council for each business unit following divisionalisation – that met on a monthly basis. PC chairs met thereafter as a separate group. Their constitution provided 'rights' to be informed and consulted by management, principally about HR matters. Managers argued their practices had become more pluralist over the 1990s. In instituting the PC system their aim initially had been to promote 'partnership and teamwork', the template being the John Lewis 'employee partnership'. The emphasis in the second half of the 1990s had shifted to 'employee representation and involvement' (HR manager interview) as the means of enlisting employees' commitment and cooperation with workplace change.

A key reason for this shift was that UNIFI had members in the branch network and from the end of the 1990s was targeting FinanceCo as potentially vulnerable under the new government's proposed statutory union recognition procedure. Management's response was to pre-empt further external involvement by organising a workforce ballot on union recognition, conducted under independent scrutiny. Employees were asked whether they wanted union recognition or representation via a PC system with greater authority. While a majority favoured the latter, around a third of the votes cast were for union recognition. The chair of the PC explains:

> There was a Staff Association, but what point there was, nobody could really see because it made absolutely no difference to the decision-making process at all. So they had a staff survey asking how would you like to be represented, would you like us to recognise a union, are you happy with what you've got, or would you like what you've got but with a bit more teeth? And that's what the majority of staff voted for.

The PC system was relaunched with a full-time officer role, a management commitment to extend the scope of consultation to business as well as HR matters and to consult at an earlier stage in the decision-making process. In addition, the company's chief executive applied his authority and, in the words of one HR manager, 'almost ordered line managers to take the partners councils seriously'. PC representatives were sponsored through employment law training so they could become involved in representing employees in grievance and disciplinary cases. This complemented a principal management objective for the PC system, union avoidance. Thus while there were managers who saw the system as a step towards the 'democratisation' of the workplace, its value for them was that it was 'not a trade union with an agenda independent of the company's' (manager interview). Their anxiety was whether employees regarded it as anything more than a 'talking shop'. This fear was exacerbated by the fact that in the rest of the Bank Group, including its own UK operations outside FinanceCo, unions are recognised. Senior managers at FinanceCo have been faced with the strategic decision of whether or not to 'fall in line' with the rest of the Group and concede union involvement, or to continue to pursue the non-union PC approach. To date, senior management have chosen the latter course. This may reflect a degree of employee relations 'path dependency' whereby any option to change from non-union to union environment would involve considerable transaction costs (Willman et al., 2003). However, within the Freeman and Medoff (1984) paradigm, the contextual algebra of employer opposition to unionism, potential union incursion and employee desire for voice makes such an employee relations regime potentially unstable. Too little independence for the PC may reinvoke union insurgence; too much may create the conditions for the absorption of the PC by union merger. As one senior manager explained:

> We have one full-time representative now who runs the Partners' Council who is paid, but one for an organisation of however many thousand people. Is that really a serious commitment? I think there's a lot more we could do to make that a far more effective way otherwise if culturally we've said we don't want to be unionised, we are in fact just really keeping the door open for a hostile unionisation to happen because if people aren't satisfied with the representation they're getting, they will eventually go and seek it somewhere else.

In terms of process, the PC also clearly plays the role of the transmission belt for management decisions and thinking, reinforcing the 'non-union' aspects of Marchington's (1994) model. The dilemmas involved in managing such a process were recognised by managers, one of whom referred to the PC as both 'immature' and 'paternalistic' in its form and content while criticising senior management for not having 'an awareness of how beneficial it (the PC) can be to create a positive environment'. The immaturity was caused by the relative lack of awareness and training of the intricacies of the employment relationship of the PC representatives, while the authoritarian paternalism is built into the structure of the PC itself. This is evidenced by the method of election of the PC chair, who was selected by the senior HR Director as one of two official candidates for election from a wider field of employee nominees previously vetted by the HR Department. The chair was then awarded a responsibility payment for an indeterminable period of tenure as well as an office next door to the HR director. The dependent nature of the PC is further evidenced by the lack of formal joint codification of decisions. Although all meetings are chaired by an elected chairperson, minutes are recorded by the personal assistant to a senior manager (often the director of finance) without recourse to amendment by the PC representatives. Crucially, there are no negotiations over pay, which remains determined centrally and unilaterally by the HR. This sense of powerlessness is best summarised by a PC representative commenting on the internal workings of the PC:

> I don't actually think we carry as much weight as we'd like, really. ... There've been instances where we've been consulted about a particular policy that's going to be changed, put forward all of our feedback and then next month the policy has actually been finalised without us actually having been consulted ... the minutes that we have taken each meeting are prepared and typed up by senior management who are distinct from Partners' Council, so when it gets actually written up the essence of what was talked about isn't relayed.

Commentators on non-union representation have drawn attention to the ability to negotiate and bargain as a real test of employee representativeness (Terry, 1999, 2003; Gollan, 2000; Lloyd, 2001). At FinanceCo, the opportunity to negotiate was limited with most meetings centred on management presentations of key business decisions followed by a discussion of the implications of these decisions. This was true of distributive issues such as pay, where management prerogative was upheld by delivering results of the pay round on an informative rather than a consultative basis. This is not to say that there was no disagreement over the substantive issues but rather that there was little scope within the structure for review or for the overturning of management imperative.

InsuranceCo

The core business has traditionally centred on the niche insurance market but the company diversified in the 1990s into the uninsured loss recovery trade. A new office was opened and in 2003 employed 120 staff. Total employment then increased to 500. The workforce includes brokers, professionally qualified solicitors who staff a legal advice service for claimants, administrative staff and call centre operatives. These workers were mostly located in the organisation's head office. A sub-office in South Wales, employing about 200 staff, specialises in claims handling. As at FinanceCo, women comprise two thirds of the employment total. And, as at FinanceCo, managers were pursuing efficiency savings and restructuring performance management systems. In 2002–3 pay bands were being displaced by competency-based pay determined through individual appraisal.

MSF, now Amicus/UNITE, had been recognised since the 1970s for the purpose of negotiating pay and conditions. Union density was around 80 per cent at the start of the 1990s, but fell thereafter. Union representatives attributed this to the expansion of employment and recruitment of individuals socialised in the Thatcher era. Few mentioned the legal proscription of closed shop agreements, although this would seem to have contributed. At the end of the 1990s management had sought and the union accepted a 'collaborative' relationship. The written agreement asserted that 'changes necessary to maintain or improve the Company's commercial success are a joint concern of managers and staff'. Management committed to provide 'the greatest possible stability of employment and earnings' and the union to 'cooperate fully in the implementation of measures designed to sustain or increase efficiency or profitability'.

As at FinanceCo, there were management concerns about the adequacy of the employee representation arrangements. Union density fluctuated around 45 per cent. Two issues had become intertwined. Did reliance on the single channel of union representation remain an effective management approach? Would it be adequate once the EU's ICE Directive was enacted? There was a European Works Council at the level of the parent organisation but no local consultation forum inclusive of all employees. HR managers discussed the logic for retaining the extant arrangements in terms of the legitimacy that the union's involvement conferred in the management of change. As one argued:

> Because if you want to get through change, let's say in terms of contract, say we want to change the shift patterns, it's much better to get the unions on board, to get them to help us through that change and then, having agreed with them, then it's binding on the whole company whether they're members or not.

Formal union–management meetings were held each quarter. The scope of the employment and HR issues considered in these and more ad hoc meetings expanded; an HR manager argued that the unions were now involved, or consulted, on all such matters. A range of direct channels of communication with employees was also in place, ostensibly matching the partnership commitment to transparency through information sharing.

Summary

Both organisations had thus reformulated their work processes and structures to include more teamworking, more responsibility, and generally higher levels of skill and work flexibility. The data recording these changes shows much similarity between the organisations in employees' perceptions of the changes in work and intensification of work in recent years. Both organisations had also moved towards introducing partnership arrangements, although the process and structure differed. In FinanceCo we can discern a shift towards NER with 'more teeth' enacted by the employer to encourage employee voice but also to continue to keep unions at bay. The resulting Partners' Council was management dominated and strongly consultative in operation. At InsuranceCo union membership had been falling, but not to a sufficient extent that the union presence could be ignored or by-passed by management. Management utilised a partnership approach to instil greater union cooperation in the management of change, and introduced a more consultative (rather than negotiative) style to enact the process.

Employees' attitudes to voice and representation

Having described the emerging employee relations regimes at the two organisations, the next task is to test the sustainability of these regimes. We attempt to do this by examining employees' perceptions of their representation channels and the effectiveness of those channels. In this way we can probe the employers' dilemma in developing voice in each of the two case study organisations. Table 3.3 below outlines employees' views of particular aspects of the effectiveness of individual voice in the two organisations. We divide our analysis into three sections – employee assessment of management communications; employee assessment of effectiveness of collective voice; and employees' preferred representation.

Employee assessment of management communications

In both organisations the amount of information given to employees about organisational change was considerable. The methods used by

Table 3.3 Employees' assessment of the extent of direct communications and involvement

	Very good (%)	Good (%)	Poor (%)	Very poor (%)	Undecided (%)
How good are your managers at keeping everyone up to date about proposed changes at work?					
FinanceCo	9	49	30	6	6
InsuranceCo	6	50	32	6	6
Union members	4	51	36	2	7
Non-members	8	49	28	10	5
How good are your managers at providing the chance to comment on changes?					
FinanceCo	6	52	28	7	7
InsuranceCo	3	42	43	5	7
Union members	0	40	45	6	9
Non-members	5	43	42	4	6
How good are your managers at responding to suggestions from employees?					
FinanceCo	3	39	37	11	10
InsuranceCo	5	46	34	2	13
Union members	2	51	32	4	11
Non-members	7	42	35	1	15
How good are your managers at involving employees in decision making?					
FinanceCo	5	37	40	6	12
InsuranceCo	6	39	38	7	10
Union members	9	38	38	6	9
Non-members	3	40	38	8	11

Note: FinanceCo, n = 128; InsuranceCo, n = 129.

management to disseminate information and receive feedback also varied, utilising both individual and collective voice mechanisms. Each of the case study organisations practised downwards communications; the use of noticeboards, staff magazines, intranet and email systems. Each had two-way communications schemes; team briefing systems that provided employee 'question time', employee attitude surveys, focus groups, opportunities for staff to quiz senior managers, and face-to-face staff appraisals. There were important differences in the ways in which the two companies managed these communications systems and attempted to integrate them with the arrangements for employees' indirect participation in decision-making. The employee interview and survey data nevertheless showed substantial similarities in the employees' experience. The survey responses are compared in Table 3.3. While a third of respondents at each organisation thought managers poor or very poor at keeping people up to date about proposed changes, employees were more likely to feel they were informed than they were to feel they were involved in decision making.

For example, at FinanceCo managers suggested they used direct communications in a structured and purposeful way. In the process they made it clear that they viewed the PC system of employee representation as one of the channels for relaying information to employees about decisions managers had made.

> Decisions are made by the decision makers who are usually the management team. ... The proposal, when it's ready for launch, goes first of all to the Partners' Council or the chair of the Partners' Council and almost at the same time ... it goes to the people affected, so they are all brought in for a face to face briefing ... They in turn are given guidelines as to how to roll out to their staff. That's the commitment bit. Staff are given a hard copy or can access it from the intranet and then give feedback ... either through the intranet, they can go to their Partners' Council representative, or they can come to line management and HR.
>
> (HR manager)

There was evidently an aim to create consent for the management agenda. It would be expected that if the partnership approach was an active process of employee involvement, then there would be positive feelings from employees that they are listened to and that managers actively solicit views. Yet many of the employees we interviewed were frustrated by the practices entailed, with just under one half of respondents saying that managers' responses to their suggestions and willingness to involve employees were 'poor' or 'very poor'. This is exemplified in comments about involvement through team meetings, team briefings and the 'fun days' or 'commitment days' organised by departmental managers.

> You see they have lots of fluffy language going on at the moment ... So they have objectives like 'having fun', saying it is an open company, but then that all goes basically to profit, doesn't it? The whole point of having that is to get the kind of atmosphere in the workplace where we're going to get most profit ... but that is touchy-feely profit.
>
> (Female professional, mortgages)

Two other criticisms of management practices recurred in the employee interviews. The first was the doubt that staff views were relayed back up the management hierarchy. Indeed, some felt their line manager's chief objective was to keep staff motivated by not explaining the pressures for higher performance they themselves were under.

> I think we've been protected a bit from what's being expected of our team leaders and the management. Basically we just get the OK, that you're needed to do this, hit these targets and sales. I'm not sure what their priority is supposed to be and why they are asking us for this or how much pressure they are under over it.
>
> (Female clerical worker, mortgages)

The second criticism was that team meetings and briefings centred narrowly on immediate operational issues. Particularly strong negative feelings were expressed in the interviews about managers' willingness to take note of concerns over substantive issues such as pay. Pay is a complex issue in the organisation, with individual performance targets linked to broadbanding developed from the Hay job evaluation and then overlaid with business division and occupational bonuses associated with the *Sharing in Success* payment scheme. *Sharing in*

Success proved to be the most contentious source of complaint, and the sense of grievance over the unfair distribution came at a series of presentations by senior management to the PC. The average management bonus was in double figures while staff bonuses varied from nothing to a single-figure amount. The management reasoning for the inequity was based on the stated premise that the management 'bore all the risk' in the organisation. After the presentation was made, there was uproar within the PC, with reports from representatives that if 'a union had been standing outside the gates now they would get busloads of members'. While PC representatives were given the opportunity to complain about the unequal distribution of the bonus, there was no provision for negotiation or review. The PC was effectively used by management to release information, with the secondary aim of allowing the PC representatives to 'let off steam' but at the same time offer some legitimation to the process of consultation and, by implication, to uphold management prerogative.

In InsuranceCo, HR managers were candid about an elision between the formal, 'open communications' policy and current practice. Authority had been devolved to departmental managers, to 'run the department in the best way they think fit' and staff communications was not always a priority. The HR department had made its own innovations, however, including the appointment of a 'dedicated' communications officer whose role was to disseminate information – about the business and HR matters – to the workforce as a whole. A stated aim was that of catering for the non-union section of the workforce. Yet the initiative instigated a dualistic arrangement that managers could use selectively. For example, the union had been informed about the major overhaul of the performance management system in 2002, while management used a focus group exercise to persuade employees of the benefits of the new pay and appraisal system. Most employee interviewees thought they received adequate information about the business. Much of this was by email and, for workers in the geographically separate ULR business in particular, reinforced the idea that senior managers were remote and of the view that

they make decisions and we're here to abide by them rather than, perhaps, 'let's discuss them and then implement them'.

(Female administrator, ULR business)

As at FinanceCo, employees felt team briefings were largely to focus attention on local performance targets. Survey participants were less likely than their FinanceCo counterparts to feel they had opportunity to comment on proposed changes (Table 3.3). Arrangements for gathering staff 'feedback' were less highly structured than at FinanceCo. On the other hand, InsuranceCo employees were the more likely to feel that managers responded to their suggestions, even though only 51 per cent of survey participants were of this view. The survey showed some differences in union and non -union members' evaluation of management, but there was no consistent pattern. Union members were not invariably the most critical.

Effectiveness of collective voice

We measure the effectiveness of collective voice in Table 3.4 by asking employees how influential they think the Partners' Council or trade union is in the organisation at representing their interests.

FinanceCo staff representatives typically compared the PC with trade union representation, or their understanding of what that might entail. In the process they divided between PC advocates and sceptics. Advocates included individuals who thought unions 'too political' and others with a vested interest in the success of FinanceCo's home-grown alternative. For the latter, it was the PC's consensual orientation that gave it a 'competitive advantage' over trade union representation, although it would seem that the appeal was aimed more at management than employees. One representative argued that

> if you take the viewpoint that you are purely here to do what the staff want, regardless of whether it's good for the company or not, then ultimately we are going to be seen as obstructive and therefore they might as well have a union because what's the difference?

Sceptics thought the PC lacked the credibility of a trade union and, as a result, was of limited interest to employees. First, it was limited to consultation and had few sanctions to hold management to the commitment to consult. To quote one representative it was 'a union that has no teeth'. Second, although the scope of consultation had increased, discussion of the distributive issues that might be thought of central interest to employees – pay, employment terms and conditions – was still largely precluded. For one representative this was the root cause

Table 3.4   Employees' assessment of partners' council/trade union influence at the workplace

	Strongly agree (%)	Agree (%)	Disagree (%)	Strongly disagree (%)	Undecided (%)
The partners' council/trade union has a lot of influence over pay					
FinanceCo	0	3	42	32	23
InsuranceCo	4	18	31	7	40
Union members	8	21	38	7	26
Non-members	1	16	26	9	48
The partners' council/trade union has a lot of influence over working conditions					
FinanceCo	3	35	32	10	20
InsuranceCo	5	29	25	1	40
Union members	11	35	30	4	20
Non-members	0	23	21	1	55
The partner's council/trade union is taken seriously by management					
FinanceCo	2	46	22	9	21
InsuranceCo	7	52	9	1	31
Union members	11	67	4	2	16
Non-members	4	40	13	1	42
The partners' council/trade union makes a difference to what it is like to work here					
FinanceCo	2	34	31	7	26
InsuranceCo	6	31	20	3	40
Union members	13	33	19	4	31
Non-members	0	29	23	3	45

Note: FinanceCo, n = 128; InsuranceCo, n = 127.

of the 'awful lot of apathy generally from staff towards the partners' council'. Third, representatives complained that the PC dealt largely with 'housekeeping issues' and issues of concern to the HR department, and that on important matters management had made 'a lot of the key decisions ... before they get to the partners council and they ask for our input'. The final and overarching criticism was that the system was not independent from management.

> Although it's written in the policies and so forth that we are an autonomous party, we're not really that autonomous because management can interfere in a lot of things.

An example was the HR department's insistence on vetting the short-list of candidates for the full-time officer role. Managers had staff representatives whose presence in the PC, many interviewees felt, dissuaded employees from voicing grievances. A professional head office worker, for example, argued that 'I think you really have to trust your partners' council rep. to not do you an injustice when representing you'.

In the interviews and questionnaire survey, employees were found to be largely sceptical of the PC's influence. The survey findings are summarised in Table 3.4. A bare 3 per cent of respondents felt the partners' council had a lot of influence over pay. Only a third (38 per cent) thought it had influence over working conditions. And since less than half (48 per cent) of respondents thought the PC was taken seriously by management it is not surprising that only a third (36 per cent) thought it 'made a difference to what it is like to work here'. Perhaps the most damning criticism was the comment of one among the clerical workers interviewed who thought the PC was 'some sort of suggestion scheme'.

InsuranceCo had union recognition, negotiated pay and a forged cooperation agreement that ostensibly made the union a partner in the management of workplace change. Union members had greater confidence in their representatives' influence in workplace management than FinanceCo employees had of their non-union PC, as is shown by the comparison of the survey findings in Table 3.4. However, on some measures the contrast was marked principally because of the limited faith PC members had in the influence wielded by their representation body. That less than a third of InsuranceCo union members (29 per cent) thought the union had a lot of influence on pay perhaps is not surprising in a period of low price inflation. Nonetheless there were union members at InsuranceCo who felt their representatives too willing to compromise in negotiations with management, while union representatives argued – somewhat fatalistically – that pay was now determined from abroad, by the parent company. The main point, however, is that the union's positive response to the company's invitation to cooperate in workplace change had not given a fillip to the union's perceived influence and the most obvious reason is that employees had experienced workplace change as benefiting principally the company. They had conceded flexibility in working time and tasks, and two-thirds of all employees surveyed felt their work had been intensified in recent years while annual pay settlements had been modest.

Most union members included in the survey (78 per cent) believed that the union was taken seriously by management. This was a clear contrast with the way in which FinanceCo PC members viewed their non-union representation body. The PC suffered from its perceived lack of independence from management. The union at InsuranceCo was not handicapped in this way but it struggled to convince members and potential members that its cooperative stance was reciprocated by influence in management. Only 46 per cent of union members in the employee survey thought the union made much difference to 'what it is like to work here'; a third (31 per cent) were undecided on the issue.

Employees' preferred representation

We have so far presented evidence that employees' attitudes towards the effectiveness of employee voice in the two organisations was marginally favourable towards their ability to be heard but generally unfavourable towards management's willingness to act on expressed concerns. This was particularly so in FinanceCo whenever substantive concerns were at stake. In InsuranceCo the majority also thought that the union was taken seriously by management, in contrast to FinanceCo where the PC was often criticised for being too heavily influenced by management. Given these differences we now probe employees' views on how they may be better represented.

In FinanceCo a majority of employees voted in 2001 to retain the PC system, although in the knowledge that it was their managers' preference and on the understanding that its influence would be strengthened. However, many of the staff representatives interviewed in 2002–3 argued that in practice little had changed, and our research found that employees in general were not convinced the PC had influence in management or were confident it could perform other representation functions. In addition, evidence from interviews would seem to confirm that such an approach was part of a conscious management strategy to neutralise the PC as an effective vehicle of employee voice. Rather, the PC was seen as a transmission belt of the management message, and representatives were expected to be lubricators of the management imperative. A mortgage specialist was particularly blunt about what she thought of the PC – 'bloody waste of time'! – on further probing, she added:

> Because it's [PC] not independent, because it is run by their own management, people won't really say 'this isn't fair' or 'this isn't right'. Nobody's got the guts to say because it's in-house.

The PC was prohibited from negotiating pay. And since pay had been individualised and made dependent on performance, as assessed at an individual appraisal by line management, it is not surprising that most surveyed employees thought they themselves or their line manager would be their best representation in securing a pay increase (Table 3.5). Relatively few surveyed employees (29 per cent) felt that PC representation was their best option for resolving a work-related grievance. As discussed earlier, its efficacy as a channel for voicing employee grievances was compromised by employee fears that their identity – as complainants – would become obvious to managers who were represented in the PC, or had access to the minutes. Indeed some staff representatives argued that in the current, relatively buoyant labour market employees were more likely to quit than attempt to secure redress for their grievances through the PC. The company sponsored staff representatives' employment law training, so that staff representation in individual grievance and disciplinary proceedings could be handled in-house. Yet there were managers who doubted that staff representatives had the confidence or expertise for the task and clearly many employees felt similarly. Only 29 per cent of survey respondents felt PC representation their best option, in the event of facing disciplinary action from managers.

In InsuranceCo union members believed the union was taken seriously by management; its *in situ* presence meant it could not be ignored. Yet union members did not perceive their representatives as having great sway in workplace management; they did not see its cooperative stance being reciprocated by management. They were more confident than their counterparts at FinanceCo in their representation body's ability to perform traditional union functions. That said, the union had acquiesced in the pay reforms introduced in 2002–3, that threatened greater individualisation of reward, and in the employee survey two-fifths of union members felt self-representation rather than union representation their best option for gaining a pay increase (Table 3.5). Workplace union representatives explained that much of their union work was about individual advocacy; organising in the workplace was not mentioned frequently.

Many managers affirmed the union's effectiveness. Line managers complained that union representatives were overly zealous in advocating the employee's case. HR managers, in contrast, valued the union's services in helping to resolve what might otherwise be difficult

Table 3.5 Employees' evaluation of who best represents them

FINANCECO	Myself (%)	Partners' Council (%)	Line Manager (%)	Undecided (%)
Who do you think would best represent you if you want to gain a pay increase?				
	33	10	49	8

	Myself (%)	Partners' Council (%)	Trade Union (%)	Undecided (%)
Who do you think would best represent you if you have a work-related grievance?				
	43	29	14	14
Who do you think would best represent you if a manager wanted to discipline you?				
	38	29	15	18

INSURANCECO	Myself (%)	Trade Union (%)	Another employee (%)	Someone else (%)
Who do you think would best represent you if you want to gain a pay increase?				
All respondents	62	30	5	3
Union members	43	50	6	1
Non-members	77	15	4	4
Who do you think would best represent you if you have a work-related grievance?				
All respondents	57	32	6	5
Union members	37	52	5	6
Non-members	72	17	7	4
Who do you think would best represent you if a manager wanted to discipline you?				
All respondents	43	47	6	4
Union members	13	83	0	4
Non-members	61	24	11	4

Note: FinanceCo, n = 128; InsuranceCo, n = 127.

and protracted disciplinary proceedings. Among union members were those who referred to representatives being on hand to 'fight for you' and 'do everything they can' for individuals in trouble at work, and 83 per cent included in the survey thought union representation their best option in the event of facing disciplinary action from management. Yet the problem for the union was convincing the majority of the workforce of the benefits of subscribing for such support.

Non-union members included those who had resigned from the union and the larger number who had never joined. Many who were interviewed argued that the union did not appear to make a difference, or a sufficient difference, to make union joining worthwhile or worth the cost. But they divided between those who felt the union did not address their needs and others who professed to feel sufficiently secure to not need the union. There were some in both groups who admitted they were 'free riders', enjoying union services – including the assurance of having a union to hand in the event of a problem at work – without paying subs.

> Well, things they do like negotiating for paid paternity leave. I benefit from that anyway. I don't have to be a member for them to negotiate that. They negotiate that as a staff benefit.
>
> (Female technician, head office)

Union density fluctuated with peaks achieved at times of crisis. For example, there had been redundancies at the ULR business in 2002, notwithstanding the 'job security' provisions of the union-management cooperation agreement. This had activated the latent demand for union representation; the union was reported to have gained members. Yet the problem was one of sustaining such membership 'surges' and retaining in the union the recent recruits. An active workplace union presence, orientated towards union organising, was required but was constrained not least by managers' conscientious application of the union facilities agreement.

Summary

We attempted to test the effectiveness of employee voice and representation both individually and collectively. We found that in both organisations the range and amount of information provided to staff about the business was considerable, and conveyed in a variety of means including team meetings and briefings, electronically, and through the employee representative channels. There is also some evidence from both organisations that employees felt positively towards management's willingness to listen to their concerns, but negatively towards management's willingness to do anything about those concerns. This was particularly the case in FinanceCo over substantive issues such as pay. In other words management heard what was being said but then brushed the concerns aside, and would appear to use communications channels simply to transmit their own message. Union members in InsuranceCo expressed the most confidence of all groups surveyed that the collective form of representation was taken seriously by management, although this was against the background of declining union influence, the presence of an increasing pool of free-riders, and management efforts to revise communication processes through the lens of partnership. We now conclude by asking ourselves why the lack of effective voice within the organisations, does union representation matter, and has partnership delivered voice for the employees?

Conclusion: Gambling with the paradox of intention

Our case study organisations share the similarity that partnership is central to the processes of employee relations. However, as Johnstone et al. (2005) have suggested analyses of partnership at the workplace need to be mindful of the contextual differences through which partnership has been isolated as a framework.

At FinanceCo partnership was enacted by management with staff consent as an alternative to union representation. As such it represents a non-union form of representation. In InsuranceCo partnership was constructed in agreement between management and union as union influence and density declined, but not to such an extent that the union could be ignored or by-passed. Our study finds that in the non-union example, FinanceCo, there were limits to the amount of involvement and influence expressed by employees through the PC machinery. Although much information was provided by managers on workplace change, there was a marked unwillingness of managers to act on employees' concerns at the effects of these changes. Employee voice, expressed as the ability of employees to persuade and invoke change, was subsequently constrained. In this respect, employee involvement was prioritised by management in its negative rather than positive sense and was used, as Ramsay (1996) has suggested in other cases, to shape employees' attitudes so that employees are more likely to accept change as the imposition of management will rather than through their own independent will. Neither has partnership been used to develop a real and equal dialogue about key aspects of the business. The PC had been constructed by management as the formal expression of non-union workplace partnership, but in reality, the PC is an ineffective agent of collective employee voice because of its dependent nature, its management dominance and its inability to move beyond the most basic consultative mechanisms. The evidence

here would support Freeman and Medoff's (1984, p. 108) original con-
tention that an effective worker voice requires that '... management
give up power and accept a dual authority channel ...' To a certain
extent, the unwillingness to release power may be historically determined by the employee relations tradition in the building society
industry whereby non-unionism has been *de rigueur*. It may also be
a product of the rule- and procedure-bound environment in financial
institutions where bad decisions can cost money and where the industry is subject to the scrutiny of external regulation. Despite these
caveats, it remains the case that management has a strategic choice over
its employee relations regime, and the choice made by management
has severely constrained the options for real employee involvement
and participatory working. We detected some discomfort within management over such a choice. Ironically, partnership is presented as a
progressive way forward for employees in the organisation with an
enhanced democracy within the workplace. But instead, the actuality
of the partnership strategy both consolidates existing power discrep-
ancies and presents only a façade of economic democracy in the
process. Rather than developing mutual gains, partnership in our case
study acts instead as a conduit for employer agendas (cf. Heckscher,
1996).

Union density had fallen at InsuranceCo to 27 per cent by 2007 but
insufficiently for the union's 'presence' to be ignored. The management
strategy was to include the union in a cooperation pact as the means
of managing workplace change. This was a largely one-way exchange
of moderation on the union's part. Coerced by interfirm competition
and the need to achieve 'added value' from the workforce, the company
was unable to concede union influence in the traditional bargaining
agenda or beyond it. Indeed, the new performance management system limited the union to negotiating the distribution of the 'pay pot'.
Union members in general remained committed to union representation although were not uncritical of their union leadership. Workplace
representatives were considered insufficiently assertive – as opposed to
incorporated – and remote so that members' involvement was passive.
The union's resources and orientation towards organising, however,
were constrained by the cooperation agreement. Non-union employees
by and large valued the union's presence as insurance. Some felt
comfortably situated not to need representation. Others articulated a
'frustrated demand' (Bryson, 2003) for effective representation. That is

to say while they wanted redress for grievances – as regards pay, workloads, equality of opportunity, management style – they did not think the gains from union membership proportionate to the charges.

Our conclusions point to a 'paradox of intention' within the non-union environment when the sought-after benefits of partnership working prove illusive as employee voice continues to be oppressed by employer antipathy to more effective employee representation. As such, our FinanceCo case study of NER-based partnership suffers from a 'paradox of intention' and becomes the reverse mirror of its own ambitions, reflecting the very opposite of its claimed democratic intent. In the union recognised case, InsuranceCo, declining union representation poses a strategic dilemma for management as it seeks to 'square the circle' between the need to encourage employee commitment as the existing representative voice mechanism goes into progressive decline. Management have sought to utilise partnership to harness employee voice (both union and non-union) and to engage employees in organisational change. Such a strategy confirms the passive portrait of partnership in the finance sector painted by Gall (2001a) whereby partnership is utilised by employers to contain union influence in an arena where union power is not sufficient to resist. However, once again, such containment of collective voice also acts to frustrate employees, who in the case of InsuranceCo demand more activism and adversarialism from their union as a result.

4

Best Value in a Local Authority

In the last two decades, public sector services have come under mounting pressure to improve performance and reduce costs in service delivery. Successive Conservative governments exposed many local public services to compulsory competitive tendering (CCT). The number of services provided by local authorities was reduced by transferring them to the private sector mainly to cut the cost of delivery. Concomitant with this change was a shift towards greater accountability to service-users together with the introduction of performance targets; factors that radically altered the framework in which public sector industrial relations operated. Following the election of New Labour in 1997, CCT was abolished. Its replacement, Best Value, far from reversing Conservative local government reforms sought to both broaden and strengthen them (Martin, 2000). Competitive tendering was no longer to be mandatory, but its coverage was extended to include all local government services. The seeming contradiction embodied in the Best Value principles of cost-saving and continuous quality improvement demanded greater control through performance indicators, training, monitoring and evaluation arrangements (Martin, 2000). Despite operational differences, in ideological terms Best Value shares much in common with the CCT regime. Competition and competitive tendering are central:

> [R]etaining work in-house without subjecting it to real competitive pressure can rarely be justified. Should an authority exercise that choice and the service fail to provide Best Value, continuing in-house provision would not be sustainable.
>
> (Cmnd 4014, 1998)

Best Value differs from CCT in one important aspect. Trade union and staff involvement is seen as important to develop the level of trust and cooperation necessary to form part of a new control mechanism for New Labour's public sector modernisation programme (Whitfield, 2001, p. 116). Best Value embraces the partnership at work agenda with its emphasis on a joint approach to service improvement. This approach focuses more on partnership as an agreement between the employer and trade unions rather than as a process involving employees. This explains why, where local authorities were adequately resourced, cooperation of trade unions is seen as key to the successful launching of Best Value pilot exercises. In practice, involvement of public service staff is marginal (Martin et al., 2001). Under Best Value partnership, in essence, is 'procedural in form, and unitary in specification' (Novitz, 2002).

The dilemma faced by public sector unions is whether to engage with partnership, and attempt to steer it towards a more pluralistic agenda, or mobilise opposition to it on the premise that its disarming nature may well leave workers defenceless against the possibility of unfavourable outcomes. Theoretical support for the partnership approach associated with Best Value can be found in Ackers (2002) and Ackers and Payne (1998). In essence they argue that the rationale underpinning partnership offers the only realistic long-term solution to the regeneration of the union movement. Ackers (2002, p. 17) contends that the potency of partnership is that it is rooted in an 'ethical agenda of social integration', contained within a new 'neo-pluralist' framework. Emphasis is placed on strengthening the links between the employment relationship, social purpose of employment and civil society. He posits that inclusion of civil society in a network of normative institutions collaborating with state regulation bodies provides a vision for taking partnership at work forward, promising a new rationale for trade unions. Critics of partnership indicate that this perspective may provide a gloss to the real nature of partnership – to secure worker accommodation behind a veil of cooperative relations – by involving unions 'in propagating managerial ideology and administering management policy' (McIlroy 2000, p. 29) in order to suppress conflict. The government has set its stall in linking with those public sector union leaderships committed to working in partnership with the government: 'Forward-looking trade unions know that the future is about partnership, and are leading the way in a number of projects' (Office of Public Service Reform 2002, p. 21).

The pressures for consensus, however, cannot hide the conflicts, tensions and contradictions inherent in the employment relationship. This explains why government preoccupations and academic concerns in combination have supported a burgeoning literature on 'partnership at work'. Few of the contributions have considered the experience of employees, in spite of the insistence in the prescriptive literature that employees are at the centre of partnership relations (Guest and Peccei, 2001). The one notable exception, a study on Best Value pilots in UK local public services, indicated negative outcomes for front line staff (Geddes, 2001). What emerged from this study were signs of reduced staffing levels, limited trade union voice, increased numerical and functional flexibility, and evidence of work intensification. This case study suggests that the early experience of Best Value has resulted in the strengthening of management's ability to restructure the labour process and employment relations to the detriment of many public sector employees. This picture complements the view that the government, in promoting the partnership agenda, is intent on achieving significant progress towards extending internal and external flexibility in both the public and private sectors (British *Fairness at Work* white paper (HMSO, 1998)).

Drawing on a single local authority case study, this chapter explores employee experiences concerning job security/insecurity, workload, job satisfaction, employee involvement and trade union representation. In the areas surveyed at the time of our research, two key services, local taxation and payroll, had just undergone Best Value reviews. By comparing and contrasting the experiences of employees in these departments with council staff employed elsewhere in the authority in areas yet to be Best-Valued, we found little evidence of positive employment outcomes from partnership. We explain this, not in terms of management failure to recognise the prerequisites for an effective partnership, but in terms of the constraints imposed by central government under which managers in the public sector operate. It is these constraints driven by New Labour's liberalising agenda that dictate the struggle to assert particular organisational priorities and goals.

The chapter is organised as follows: First we examine the part played by trade unions at the local level in cooperating with the introduction and establishment of Best Value and workplace partnership. Next we explore trade union members' view of their unions' role and influence at the workplace. Third, we evaluate the impact of Best Value on job security, work intensification and job satisfaction. Fourth, attention is directed towards employee involvement, as improvements in consultation and participation in management decision-making are included in the TUC's list of essential principles in partnership arrangements and within the Best Value 'ethos' (TUC, 2001). Finally, a conclusion summarises and interprets findings within a critical industrial relations framework.

The research, conducted in 2001, used a mix of quantitative and qualitative data collection techniques to assemble employees' experiences at a local authority (CityCo) with 18,500 staff. Membership of the largest trade unions, UNISON, T&GWU and GMB totalled around 4000, 800 and 700 respectively. Taped interviews were carried out with four representatives from these unions and one UCATT representative. At the workplace, taped interviews were conducted with 22 senior and line managers, and 62 staff employed in a variety of occupations in several key services staffed by around 3235 employees. Survey questionnaires were distributed to a sample of staff across these services.[1] In all, 747 questionnaires were distributed and 389 completed, a response rate of 52 per cent. In the Best-Valued areas (local taxation and payroll) 30 interviews were conducted and 148 questionnaires distributed, of which 89 were returned, a 60 per cent response rate.

The role of local trade unions

New Labour's view that partnership relations and practices between employers and employees lead to improved organisational performance and greater employment security has been strongly supported by the TUC (2001). The guiding principles for partnership and joint working on Best Value were set down in an agreement between the national employers and the recognised trade unions (GMB, T&GWU, UNISON) in the National Joint Council Framework (NJCF) agreement (2000). This agreement conferred institutional legitimacy on union involvement in the Best Value process and despite unease among UNISON activists that the government was putting cost before quality, unions remained critically supportive (Geddes, 2001; Martin et al., 2001). The existence of two-tier workforces in local government-contracted outservices was of greater concern (UNISON, 2002) than partnership outcomes associated with the TUC's list of essential principles. In respect to Best Value pilot runs, Geddes (2001) found that generally the level of trade union involvement was much greater at national level than at local level. The situation we encountered in our case study was less clear. Throughout most of the 1980s and 1990s, the trade unions had a good relationship with the local authority management at our research site. CityCo for most of this period was Labour-controlled, as it was at the time of our research. In 1996, it became a unitary authority consisting of 35 wards, with 70 elected councillors responsible for delivering the full range of local council services. In 2000, CityCo adopted a cabinet structure comprising a Cabinet Office and five departments: Education and Lifelong Learning; Environment, Transport and Leisure; Neighbourhood and Housing Services; Social Services and Health; Central Support Services. New personnel policies had been introduced, such as positive action in recruitment of people from ethnic minority groups, as part of its policy to promote equality. In partnership with the trade unions, different work-life balance schemes had been introduced. The unions were keen to maintain their collaborative relationship. Interviews with local full-time representatives of the main unions (UNISON, T&GWU and GMB) revealed that they were heavily involved in the discourse and practice of partnership and Best Value at CityCo, a strategy in which they were all united.

Full-time lay officials of the unions, enthused by the election of a Labour government in 1997, supported the replacement of CCT with Best Value. But a more guarded oppositional approach was adopted when it became clear that the performance levels and organisational processes set by Best Value reviews forced the local authority to consider outsourcing services if it was unable to get the service improvements required in-house. This development served to deepen the involvement of the unions in Best Value steering groups, as the following comment from a UNISON full-time lay official affirms:

> It's become more and more obvious that it's [Best Value] really an outsourcing exercise, then we got angrier and angrier about it. But at the same time we tried to emphasize the need of getting a trade unionist on every steering group and with the other unions we've worked to do that.

These steering groups usually comprised 12 council officials and three union representatives (who were usually full-time lay officials). Their role was to find ways to improve services by sharing best practice, and identifying and correcting deficiencies. By participating in steering groups, trade union officials could attend Best Value review panel meetings. One of the responsibilities of these panels was to assess whether the public would be better served by externalising services or keeping them in-house. The unions' strategy was to secure a more powerful voice on these bodies to gain more leverage in respect to decisions regarding the implementation of Best Value and the associated changes to the labour process, job security and quality of working life. Criticism of Best Value *per se* was directed at central rather than local government. A T&G full-time lay official outlined and justified this strategy in these words:

> I much prefer our people be involved in trying to lead the debate where we want it to go and achieve what we want to achieve in terms of defending our members, rather than be on the outside looking in and have no influence, because it seems to me you can get involved in a process and if it looks like it's bad news, you can withdraw. Personally I'm not sure if I'd advocate that, because if it looks like it's being nasty it seems to me there's even more reason to be involved in it, because you could be into some form of damage limitation type exercise.

As well as a 'damage limitation exercise' the unions' rationale for involvement in Best Value and partnership included taking into account the interests of a wider constituency of 'stakeholders'. At face value this appears to reflect partnership as outlined by Ackers's (2002) 'neo-pluralist' stand. This is how a full-time lay official described it:

> The first point is that you have to accept that the reason why we're here in the local authorities is to provide services to the people of [the City]. That's fundamentally the point, because without those people to provide the services for, we don't exist ...
>
> So the partnership arrangement becomes, as a matter of Best Value process, not just about the interaction between management and union, it's about management and union, management and staff

who might not be a member of the union, it's about management and public.

This commitment to cementing the links between union activity, paid work and wider society resonates with the idea that an alternative industrial relations regime could be developed based on social cohesion between trade unions, local communities and local and central government. However, missing from this equation is public service workers' involvement in and experience of new ways of working under the Best Value regime. According to one senior personnel manager the trade unions had 'an almost paternal approach to saying well we know what's best for the workforce and indeed for the council.' While one full-time lay official maintained that the way the development of partnership working as part of Best Value

> manifested itself very much along the lines of institutions and almost, in some areas management say, 'as long as I've spoken to [you the full-time union official], then I've spoken to all of those people as well, because you are the representative'.

Full-time lay officials were concerned with defending traditional aspects of the employment relationship, particularly job security and pay. They regarded the attainment of mooted partnership outcomes such as job satisfaction and employee involvement as secondary, 'a bonus … in terms of the ever decreasing budget situation'. There was an acceptance, albeit grudgingly, that the frontier of control had shifted towards management and the process of employee involvement was restricted to increased consultation. Keeping services in-house was regarded as the best way to defend existing jobs and levels of pay. Echoing the national policy of their respective unions, local trade unions secured support from local authority managers responsible for coordinating the implementation of Best Value:

> Some of the local tax managers were absolutely excellent in the process and if the city council wants to have a look at a process in terms of Best Value where you've got management and unions working together to achieve an end, which in this case was to make sure that the city council maintained control of the operation, I don't think you'll find a better example.

The shift of the centralised and institutional form of industrial relations arrangements to local authority level served to expedite union engagement with Best Value. Senior management at CityCo worked with the local union hierarchy to hammer out restructuring plans to achieve service improvements designed to meet Best Value requirements and keep services in-house. The problem for unions in pursuing this strategy was that this could put them in a weakened position (due to their complicity in the implementation of Best Value) to effectively join or organise a campaign against Best Value, if the changes that it brought about turned out to be detrimental to CityCo's workforce. Union officials were aware of this:

> There's a difficulty with being involved in it [Best Value] so far as if you're involved and it goes wrong, you can be seen as being complicit with it.

By joining forces with managers in Best Value panels and steering groups, local unions continued to service their members at arms length. The emphasis the unions placed on working closely with the employers was grounded on the well-embedded cooperative relationship the unions had with CityCo. Therefore, initially, this policy of cooperation with local authority management in engaging with Best Value was not seen as particularly contentious. The thought of mobilising union membership in opposition to Best Value, or developing union participation, at the local level, was never envisaged, which left the bargaining position of union officials very weak. In these circumstances the workforce was in a highly vulnerable position and options other than compliance to service improvement plans, based on keeping services in-house, were limited, as the remarks by a local taxation employee suggest:

> They [management] were putting all these measures together to make it [the service] cheaper and the unions went along with it because they didn't agree with services being out-sourced. We had a union meeting that clashed here and ... [the union representative] said 'well I'm not concerned about June 2002 all I'm concerned about is the moment [2001] and securing your jobs with CityCo as your employer'. They'll worry about that when they come across it. But I just think a lot of people will be out

of work and I really wouldn't like to be one of those people that are left.

Our survey asked a series of questions that explored employee perceptions of the trade unions' role and influence in the workplace. In respect to two specific questions union potency was more apparent in non-Best-Valued departments than in those that had undergone Best Value reviews. Notably, in response to the statement 'unions make a difference to what it is like to work here', trade union members in the two Best Value departments surveyed were less convinced that this was the case (45 per cent agreed or strongly agreed) than their colleagues in non Best-Valued departments (54 per cent agreed or strongly agreed). A similar result was returned in response to the question whether unions have a lot of influence over working conditions. Only 39 per cent of respondents in Best Value departments agreed or strongly agreed that they felt that this was the case compared to 50 per cent in non-Best-Valued departments. Therefore, it is not surprising to find that 61 per cent of union members in non-Best-Valued departments agreed or strongly agreed that they felt loyal to their trade union compared to 48 per cent in Best Value departments. The view of one local taxation employee and trade union member captures the opinion of many working in this department:

> I don't think there's any advantage being in the union. There's no difference whether you're a union member or not. Now I've stayed a union member because they look after me individually. I suppose it's somewhere to go and at least I can get some representation or legal advice or whatever.

We turn now to consider the implications, for employees, of the union strategy undertaken. First we look at job insecurity, work intensification and job satisfaction.

Security of employment, the intensification of work and job satisfaction

> I see Best Value as the biggest threat to jobs in local government that there's ever been, with the possible exception of competitive tendering.
>
> (CityCo, T&G full-time official)

> We thought Best Value was a good thing and would open up oppor-
> tunities but as things have developed we have changed our mind.
> We are now in fear of Best Value and associate it with Downsizing.
> (CityCo, Business Development Manager)

Our data suggest that union officials were right to perceive Best Value
as a catalyst powerful enough to raise the spectre of job insecurity,
despite union efforts to counter such an outcome through its involvement strategy. Interviews with CityCo staff suggest that their understanding of job insecurity is similar to the definitions on employment
and job insecurity provided by Standing (1999,cited in Burchill, 2002,
p. 63). Job insecurity refers to dismissal, layoff, short time, job redesign
and job redeployment.

Best Value reviews, and the subsequent restructuring and reorganisation of work, triggered feelings of job insecurity. Some of the staff
interviewed in payroll, one of the departments subjected to a Best Value
review, expressed concern that managers were playing on employees'
sense of job insecurity by regular announcements about the threat of
outsourcing:

> We keep on being told about this firm or that firm out there who
> wants to take the business away from the Council. You know,
> they're all going to outsource it or, you know, bring in firms who
> are gonna come in and take the payroll away.

Another payroll employee reported that a reduction in core staff followed the implementation of Best Value: 'they just cut and cut staff
and we just had to cope and do it.' Increasingly, payroll relied on
temporary and agency staff due to the uncertainty about future job
security under the Best Value regime. This was a different strategy to
that carried out at local taxation, the second Best Value department.
Here, once it was decided that the service was to be retained in-house,
temporary workers, widely used in the period of uncertainty, were
given an opportunity to apply for a limited number of jobs on a permanent contract. The idea was that the infusion of new blood would
accelerate acceptance of change or induce long-term members of staff
to volunteer for redundancy.

The view of many local taxation staff was that despite the difficulties
of covering the main contents of the job 'at the end of the day they're

going to have to cut people because that's the budget they've got'. None the less, the general feeling was that concerns about job security would be even greater if the service was outsourced. CityCo's redeployment policy was flagged up as an important lifeline to those employees identified as surplus to requirement. However, insecurity also stems from redeployment due to diminished career progression prospects and the subsequent impact on the chances of pay advancement by moving through the pay scales. As one local taxation officer observed:

> In the last ten years I've had five different [Council] jobs and any one of them hasn't been through choice. They've all been redeployments ... Now I got this job permanently in November 2000 and in June 2002 we'll have another review and there's going to be dramatic job cuts in the implementation of the service work plan.

This insecurity was also recognised by CityCo's head of property and financial services:

> Now these are people [local taxation staff] with good career, good track records, probably doing this for 20 years and yet they find themselves in a redundancy situation where it is quite difficult to say, 'well what's the outside market for these skills?'

Job insecurity was also perceived in non-Best-Valued departments but often it was tied to the thought that they would soon be in line for a review, with the possibility that their work might be outsourced. For example, one employee commented:

> Curiously, under CCT, at the time the tenders were let, there was always a fear about the job and job security; because you either won it or you didn't ... Best Value, curiously, has made it worse because the fear a lot of people have is that almost at any time, the client can say, sorry you're no longer giving us best value, we're going to change the contractor. It's fairly clear cut, CCT, you're either cheapest or you're not, Best Value is an element of subjectivity I suppose.

This aside, the dominant view in these non-Best-Valued departments was that although local authority jobs are not as secure as they had been, job security was 'reasonable now compared with the private sector'.

Table 4.1 presents employees' views on job security taken from the questionnaire survey. It compares employees' views on job security in Best-Valued and non-Best-Valued departments. The results show that many staff in Best-Valued departments are particularly concerned about the effects of job insecurity.

In the non-Best-Valued departments surveyed, 62 per cent of the non-managerial staff agreed or strongly agreed that they felt their job was secure. In sharp contrast, only 40 per cent of staff in Best-Valued departments did so. Moreover, only 41 per cent of the latter indicated that they thought their managers were good or very good at maintaining the job security of council employees, compared to 57 per cent of staff surveyed in non Best-Valued departments.

Work intensification

Shifts in the organisation of work and staff utilisation precipitated, for many employees, significant increases in work intensification, especially in the Best-Valued departments. The Best Value review in the local taxation department involved a market-testing process and as a consequence an explicit threat of service externalisation. Management

Table 4.1   CityCo's employees' views (excluding managers) on job security: Comparison between Best-Valued and non-Best-Valued departments

Department	Strongly agree/ Agree (%)	Disagree/ Strongly disagree (%)	Undecided (%)
*I feel my job is secure in this workplace**			
Best-Valued departments	40	47	13
All other surveyed departments	62	28	10
	Very good/ Good (%)	**Poor/Very poor (%)**	**Undecided (%)**
How good are your managers at maintaining the job security of Council employees?			
Best-Valued departments	41	30	29
All other surveyed departments	57	25	18

Note: n = 342; *Chi-square test significant at the 0.05 level.

were divided over whether the service should be outsourced or kept in-house with the directorate supporting the former and the local taxation manager supporting the latter. The outcome was to retain the service in-house based on the implementation of a seven-year service improvement plan. Undoubtedly, the support provided by the trade unions influenced the final decision, as the local taxation manager confirmed:

> We were enormously helped by our relationships with the trade unions. The key players in our consultation were Transport & General and Unison and they were extremely pragmatic, helpful, everything. Very supportive and have continued to be helpful.

The main reason for keeping the service in-house was that after completion of the bidding process it became clear that compared with the internal bid, based on the seven-year plan, externalisation would not yield a significant saving in cost. The service improvement plan involved gradually reducing the numbers employed in local taxation staff. Generic working (multitasking), a policy first introduced in 1997, would continue but in a modified form.[2] Customer focus teams were established in order to clear the volume of work that had built up in certain areas. Membership of these teams was based on a monthly rota system and involved staff taking on a wide range of specialist taxation roles; commercial business rates, council tax billing, council tax collection and tax recovery. In addition, these teams helped to roster a new 'call centre' for service users. In short, the Best Value process catalysed a significant increase on an already heavy workload. A local taxation manager, under pressure to meet aggressive performance targets, recognised the impact this was having on staff:

> [That staff] were asked to become all singing/all dancing people and a lot of people actually were down-graded during the restructure and now they've moved into a huge technological change ... Performance targets, individual performance targets and a requirement of trying to communicate to them ... that you will never be in an unchanging environment again. This is the pace at which, we must accept, we all have to work at because whilst there is the requirement for continuous improvement, that will naturally lend itself to continual change.

The introduction of dedicated customer service teams; a new computer-based document management system (scanning and storing documents electronically); windows-based personal computers; online payment facility; and extended opening times was accompanied with monitoring, performance testing and target setting. Staff were expected to complete a preset amount of work per day. And following the introduction of generic working and the establishment of dedicated customer service teams, targets were gradually increased and every 'single second of the day' had to be justified.

Apropos performance monitoring, our survey revealed there was a greater belief among employees in Best Value departments that the employee development review (EDR) was more of a performance appraisal than an opportunity for the employee to discuss career development plans. In response to the probe 'the EDR used to help me with my career development' only 26 per cent of Best Value employees indicated in the affirmative compared to 31 per cent in non Best-Valued departments. More tellingly, 40 per cent of Best Value employees said that EDR meetings were used to monitor work performance compared to 31 per cent in non Best-Valued departments. One local taxation officer interviewed commented that performance assessment was an integral part of the EDR:

> Yes you've got targets and they talk about whether you meet those targets, not for me but at your level, the amount of work you get through in a day. You've got x pieces of post, you got an error rate as well.

And another observed that career development was a peripheral part of the EDR agenda:

> Yes. I don't think its so much career aspirations is it?

A payroll manager expressed that she did not 'intend to do other than constantly monitor the whole floor, even though my job actually is to monitor my pool'.

Staff in payroll indicated that the Best Value review was a somewhat clandestine affair. As in local taxation the directorate favoured outsourcing the service, while payroll management fought and won to keep it in-house. Staff were ill-informed and as one officer remarked kept 'very much in the dark'. There was little information coming through union channels. Although payroll passed the Best Value review, according to one line manager 'other than a few one liners that may have been thrust at them, it was never gone into in that much depth. It's just that, yes, we came through it, we carry on now'. Staff certainly felt the impact of the review; downsizing, the use of temporary and agency staff, and cost cutting precipitated increases in intensive work effort. A moratorium on the recruitment of permanent staff led to an increase in the use of agency and temporary staff. While to a limited degree this externalised job insecurity, it intensified the work of permanent staff, as they had to monitor and manage the work of temporary and agency staff. As one payroll officer reported:

> It's [the workload] accumulating all the time, and the approach too which is to drag a few temporary staff in to do the job. But the problem there is obviously, you know, drag a few temporary staff in, they need to be trained up, that impacts on me.

A line manager acknowledged the increase in work but she remarked that 'even if they feel that they are working harder ... the initial consolation is that everybody else on the same grade is working equally hard.' In effect this put 'the ills of work back on the shoulders of those fellow "victims"' (Sennett, 1998, pp. 115–16).

Our quantitative survey data indicate that most employees perceived work had intensified at CityCo, especially in the Best-Valued areas, as Table 4.2 demonstrates. The proportion of staff indicating that the increase in the amount of work they were expected to complete each week, compared to three years ago, was significantly greater in Best-Valued departments than was the case in non-Best-Valued departments.

Job satisfaction

Although other sections of this chapter touch on issues relating to job satisfaction, for example job security and employee involvement, this section examines two specific intrinsic factors, level of job influence and sense of achievement relating to the quality of working life. Table 4.3 compares these two key aspects across Best-Valued and non Best-Valued departments.

Table 4.2 Employees' experience (excluding managers) of work intensification at CityCo: Comparison between Best-Valued and non-Best-Valued departments

	Increased (%)	Decreased (%)	Unchanged (%)
Change to the amount of work I am expected to complete each week*			
Best-Valued departments	75	3	22
All other surveyed departments	59	4	37

Note: n = 342; *Chi-square test significant at the 0.05 level.

Table 4.3 Employee job satisfaction (excluding managers): Comparison between Best-Valued and non-Best-Valued departments

Department	Very satisfied/ Satisfied (%)	Dissatisfied/ Very dissatisfied (%)	Undecided (%)
How satisfied are you with the amount of influence you have over your job?*			
Best-Valued departments	41	53	6
All other surveyed departments	61	31	8
How satisfied are you with the sense of achievement you get from your work?			
Best-Valued departments	44	48	8
All other surveyed departments	63	29	8

Note: n = 342; *Chi-square test significant at the 0.05 level.

The majority of the staff employed in Best-Valued departments indicated that they were dissatisfied with the amount of influence they had over their job. In contrast, the majority of the staff in non Best-Valued departments indicated they were satisfied in this respect. Dissatisfaction was particularly prevalent among local taxation officers. The service improvement plan removed much of the influence this group felt they had over their job:

> We have no control over our work at all now. We are told that we will work on post for this two week period or you will work on a report of, I don't know maybe liability order cases, then we move on to the next recovery stage for the next few weeks.
>
> (local taxation officer)

Similarly, only just over two-fifths of staff in Best-Valued departments expressed that they were satisfied or very satisfied with the sense
of achievement they got from their work, while markedly nearly two-
thirds of non Best-Valued staff did so. Again local taxation officers
fared badly on this measure:

> Now, because of the way the work is issued, it used to be you had
> your area and you used to deal with that, now its a question of
> okay all this work needs to be done so you just get given a pile of
> work. You probably have no knowledge of the area of any of the
> people within it so you don't get the satisfaction of following that
> through at all.

And the following comments echo the dissatisfaction of the majority
of payroll staff:

> I used to come into work on a Monday morning and enjoy, you
> know, enjoy the company, the actual whole feel of the place.
> Everybody seemed to be working to the same goal; we were all work-
> ing as a team ... These days, it seems the team atmosphere's gone.
> Everybody seems to be working for themselves these days; again
> that's partly due to the amount of work every individual's got.

Employee involvement

The principle that councils should 'allow unions to become one of
the architects of change' was an important aspect of Best Value working provided by the National Joint Council Framework agreement.
Advocates of partnership argue that advantages will be forthcoming
for both employers and employees if staff are more involved in organisational decision making and employers and trade unions work
together in cooperation. Staff will benefit from a relationship based
on greater trust (Guest and Peccei, 2001; Makin et al., 1996, pp. 234,
276–7). But the readiness of councils to involve employees was geared
more towards facilitating change than empowering them in the decision making process. Our findings, similar to Geddes (2001), show that
employee participation under Best Value was more about downward
communication than engaging employees in a two-way dialogue about

change. Table 4.4 shows that employee involvement in decision making was perceived to be poor or very poor across the departments we surveyed. Staff in Best-Valued departments, however, registered more negative scores than did non-Best-Valued departments. One local taxation administrator observed: 'we were involved [in the service improvement plan]. We were asked questions. But I don't think our decision or our input had anything to do with the [final] decision.' Local taxation employees sensed that their views were 'filtered' or 'vetoed', consequently they felt excluded from the decision-making process.

The results from our survey presented in Table 4.4 suggest that managers in Best-Valued departments were perceived to be much better at communicating with their staff than their counterparts in non Best-Valued departments. Employees' evaluation of how good their managers were at keeping everyone up to date about proposed changes

Table 4.4   Employees' evaluation (excluding managers) of how good managers are at employee communications and involvement: Comparison between Best-Valued and non-Best-Valued departments

Department	Very good/ Good (%)	Poor/ Very poor (%)	Undecided (%)
Involving employees in decision-making			
Best-Valued departments	27	64	9
All other surveyed departments	35	56	9
*Keeping everyone up to date about proposed changes at work**			
Best-Valued departments	57	31	12
All other surveyed departments	45	49	6
Providing everyone with the chance to comment on proposed changes			
Best-Valued departments	49	41	10
All other surveyed departments	38	55	7
Responding to suggestions from employees			
Best-Valued departments	34	53	13
All other surveyed departments	33	55	12

Note: n = 342; *Chi-square test significant at the 0.01 level.

at work was significantly superior in Best-Valued departments than in non-Best-Valued departments. Moreover, almost half of staff in Best-Valued departments signalled that managers were good or very good at providing employees with the chance to comment on proposed changes against 38 per cent of non-Best-Valued staff. Best-Valued and non-Best-Valued departments were evenly divided on the question 'how good are managers at responding to suggestions from employees', with only one-third of all respondents returning a positive score. These results highlight our view that Best Value is more to do with facilitating change than empowering employees in the organisational decision-making process.

Certainly the local taxation employees we interviewed confirmed that communications had improved, although this was not the case for payroll employees. It seems that local taxation was an exemplar case in respect to information-provision related to the Best Value process:

> I don't think you can fault the amount of communications that are in place. Getting information from the top down there are a number of methods and that you feel perhaps there is maybe too much of it because there is a bit of this information overload. But it's all about being open with staff and keep the staff informed. You know, 'we've got nothing to hide, we want you to know what's going on' and then we can comment and have feedback (local taxation officer).

The better ratings local taxation received in respect to communication were largely, but not solely, based on cascading information downwards. In local taxation, the senior manager briefed line managers three times a week. These were formal briefings, and minutes were taken and distributed to all staff to keep them abreast of changes and issues. Line managers were also involved in contingency meetings and project groups, so they were well informed to brief their staff at monthly section meetings. Complementing these methods of communication was the Office Committee comprising representatives of management and staff (union and non-union) across local taxation. The main purpose of this committee was to bring together ideas and suggestions from staff to discuss and decide whether or not they were worth pursuing. The overwhelming view elicited from interviewees was that this committee was slow to respond and not very effective. Despite the array of communication methods, the flow was largely one way, downwards with meaningful employee voice largely absent. Forums and technology (email) were available to staff to voice their views but as one senior taxation officer remarked: 'we get feedback but the feedback would be that will happen anyway … it's almost turning into a bit of a dictatorship in this is what's happening regardless of whether its right or wrong.'

In payroll, while some sections had monthly staff meetings, others did not. Minutes of these meetings were passed on to senior managers but some employees expressed discontent that feedback from these minutes was not always forthcoming. Line managers, however, felt overwhelmed with information they received both in hard copy and electronic formats. They did not have time to digest it and pass on information to their staff:

> OK, I'll do the reading in my lunch hour. But, then, sometimes you don't have a lunch hour. OK, I'll do it in the evening. Well, then that means you've got to leave early enough to go home and do the reading. It's, which one are we going to do here? Because you've got to do the reading to know what's going on; you can't tell the people what's going on if you don't what is going on yourself.

Problems with communications in payroll clearly stemmed from the increasing workloads of line managers.

Conclusion

Best Value was implemented with a clear set of objectives – 'a duty to deliver services to clear standards – covering both cost and quality – by the most effective, economic and efficient means available' (Cmnd 4014, 1998). This could only be achieved, however, by increasing labour productivity through new ways of working. To deliver service improvement, therefore, a new control mechanism was necessary to secure the cooperation of the workforce. Workplace partnership was seen by the policy makers as the way in which to garner support from public service staff and their unions. Traditional bureaucratic centralised forms of management–union relationships were replicated at the local level, and utilised to forge such an arrangement at CityCo.

The main public sector unions at CityCo, not wishing to be marginalised, decided that the best way to protect jobs was to grasp the nettle of Best Value and become involved in review panels and steering groups with local authority management. The strategy was aimed to keep public services in-house, an objective shared by managers in the departments selected to run Best Value pilots.

Union members in the Best-Valued departments remained passive and detached from this form of participation, despite being well informed of the changes (for variations in union strategy in the public sector see Danford et al., 2003, pp. 124–7). This provision of information on work organisation change was more to do with improving managerial effectiveness than engendering employee involvement. Employee compliance to Best Value practices was achieved through agreements to changes in working practices with the local public service unions. The irony is that the aim of the unions to protect jobs was not achieved. The belief that jobs were insecure was significantly higher in Best-Valued than non-Best-Valued areas. This belief was borne out in local taxation. By June 2002, staff numbers here had reduced from 134 to 104.5 full-time equivalent positions. The long-term plan (2004–5) was to further reduce the Service to 77 staff (Audit Commission, 2002). If service improvement plans under Best Value underachieve, the likelihood is that these services will be contracted out. Roper et al. (2007) reveal the role of the Audit Commission in constraining the ability of trade unions to protect their members' interests through the collective bargaining process. The threat to externalise services if the Audit Commission deems that unsatisfactory progress has been made in delivering Best Value compounds the difficulties that trade unions have in resisting heightened job security and work intensification. Subsequent to our research in December 2003, maintenance services for CityCo's public parks were given to a new private contractor. The prospect, therefore, is for further increases in work intensification and more job insecurity. The rate of increase in intensive work effort was, at the time of our research, already significantly greater in Best-Valued departments than in non-Best-Valued departments. These are some of the realities of Best Value. Employee benefits associated with partnership at work in Best-Valued areas were no better than non-Best-Valued areas and, in some cases, significantly worse, for instance job security, job satisfaction and the intensification of work.

Despite the cooperative character of local industrial relations that provided a favourable environment for the introduction of Best Value and workplace partnership, this case study found little evidence to support a move towards 'social cohesion' emphasised in partnership discourse. This discourse fails to take full account of the outcome of partnership for most workers. In this case study, unions, in the face of the requirements imposed by central government that Best Value must deliver cost reductions and quality improvement, accepted that it was unlikely that quality of working life issues, such as job satisfaction, would feature very highly. Union involvement in Best Value was aimed to augment its effort to keep public services in-house and to protect the jobs of core workers. Unions succeeded in retaining services but were less successful in protecting jobs. Concern with other employment issues, such as work intensification, remained secondary. Unions had low expectations of CityCo delivering on favourable workplace partnership outcomes so the returns for union accommodation are even more negative. Accommodation to the new politico-economic pressures was not the only way open to trade unions, since interview data suggest that unions did not consider alternative strategies.

One such alternative approach, documented elsewhere, is premised on a somewhat more sceptical view of union–management involvement processes, known as 'engage and change' (Stewart and Wass, 1998). This goes to the heart of new management strategies aimed at managing change on terms favourable to the employer. This is crucial since, if one is committed to a pluralistic approach, then it would seem obvious that variant accounts of change may arise. These would necessarily go beyond robust rhetoric, since they would anticipate and depend on employee mobilisation. There is a clue in our data as to what it may be that employees feel would represent focus of attention. Our results highlight that communication was seen as top down, reflecting the employers' need to give voice to interests not always entirely to employees' liking. Critical issues around which a union 'engaging to change' agenda might be developed include planning to avoid intensification of work; a positive quality of working life agenda based on tight scrutiny of stress levels premised on a rejection of a long-hours culture; employee involvement at team level on all dimensions linked to workplace change, but with union involvement independent of management scrutiny. It might not solve the issue of outsourcing, but it would allow employee scope to anticipate job reduction and the ability to plan union action to block most of it, together with increased stress and the diminution of the quality of working life more broadly.

This case study indicates that it is important for unions to seek alternative and more participative forms of resistance to New Labour's Best Value regime if the deterioration in public service workers' employment prospects and employment conditions is to be arrested. Far from introducing a new 'neo-pluralist' paradigm based on mutual gain, partnership poses real dangers to employees and their unions, should cooperation and consensus become vehicles for work intensification and job loss.

5
Partnership on Prescription in the NHS

Labour governments since 1997 have embraced 'partnership at work' as central to their agenda for industrial relations 'modernisation'. Their efforts to influence private sector employers' practices have been criticised as light touch (e.g. Terry, 2003). A heavier hand has been applied in the public services sector, however, and in the NHS in particular, in the context of the reforms Labour ministers have rolled out under the banner of NHS 'modernisation' (Martínez Lucio and Stuart, 2002). It is, therefore, relevant to ask whether NHS employees have experienced partnership as increased direct and union-mediated involvement in organisational decision-making, or simply as exhortation to be more hard working and committed to employer and government-prescribed service improvement targets. In this chapter, we use 'evidence based research' amassed at one NHS hospital trust in 2002 to explore employees' experiences of the staff involvement and partnership working agenda that the Department of Health developed from the late 1990s.

Public policy context

The Labour Party made high-profile electoral commitments in 1997 to achieve improvement in the quality of NHS services, as opposed to efficiency savings alone. Labour accepted the devolved NHS organisational structure that was the legacy of 1979–97 Conservative administrations, but pledged initially to retreat from the 'marketisation' reforms of the 1990s and to encourage cooperation among service providers in ways that would exploit available scale economies. In the run up to the

2001 general election, Labour ministers committed substantially higher levels of public expenditure to the health service for succeeding years. Already, however, they had given the green light for increased private sector involvement. This has developed to include the delivery of clinical services (the independent sector treatment centre programme) in addition to the management of ancillary and administration functions outsourced by NHS organisations (the shared services initiative and, more recently, practice-based commissioning) and the financing of new capital projects (hospital facilities leased to the NHS for annual 'unitary' payments, under the Private Finance Initiative). The publication in 2004 of a national price list for NHS treatments – delivered by NHS or by private healthcare organisations as part of a 'payment by results' system in which 'the money followed the patient' – apparently reinstated (in more assertive form) the 1990s Conservative governments' 'internal market' reforms (Shifrin, 2004).

In short, while the Labour government has proclaimed at successive general elections that the NHS is safe in its hands, over successive terms of office it has made more rapid strides with NHS privatisation and marketisation than the Conservative administrations of the 1980s and 1990s that articulated an anti-public sector ideology (Givan and Bach, 2007; Pollock, 2007). Labour ministers have employed the rhetoric of pragmatism ('whatever works') and of 'patient choice' to push their reforms through, irrespective of the opposition mounted by public sector unions and organised NHS user groups.

The *NHS Plan* published by the Department of Health in 2000 delineated the parameters of the 'modernisation' programme (as envisaged at that time). Its subtitle – a plan for investment, a plan for reform – made clear that the government expected reciprocation from NHS staff, unions and managers for the public investment being ploughed in; that is, cooperation in reforms of working practices, working time patterns and modes of delivering NHS services that would add up to 'higher performance'. In order to exact the performance improvements, the Labour government relied in its first two terms of office on the regime that had been set in place by the 1992–7 Conservative administration (described by Stuart and Martínez Lucio, 2000, as one of 'naming and shaming'.) Performance targets were set centrally, there was annual audit of service provider organisations against these and the results were published in national 'league tables'. Trust management performance was assessed against financial, patient service and human resource management (HRM) targets.

HRM attained a much higher profile in NHS strategy than previously, in part because endemic recruitment and retention difficulties threatened the capacity of provider organisations to deliver services – let alone targeted performance improvements. At the centre of the NHS–HR strategy, however, were the proposals for long-term reform of pay and grading that (in principle) would provide trust managers with greater flexibility in labour deployment secured through the integration of occupational pay structures and revision of 'unsocial hours' payments (Winchester, 2005). The *Agenda for Change* agreement took some time to secure; negotiations involving the leaderships of the professional and TUC affiliated unions represented in the extant Whitley Council and Pay Review body structures for national pay determination continued from 1999 to 2004.

Staff involvement and partnership working were central to the national HR strategy. The Department of Health's *Working Together* HR framework in 1998 prescribed the development of an 'involving culture' and set targets for managers and a timescale for their achievement. It was followed by a succession of publications (1999, 2002, 2003) that cited 'evidence based research' to make persuasive the case that direct employee involvement in organisational decision-making achieved 'win-win' outcomes; a better quality of working life for employees, a more motivated and productive workforce for managers and one attuned to focusing treatment on the individual patient's needs. Conservative governments in the 1990s introduced a charter of 'patient rights' (defined by government centrally) as the means of exacting quantitative performance improvement from NHS staff (reduced patient 'waiting time' for treatment). The staff involvement and partnership working agenda from the late 1990s was presented as reconstructing NHS 'good employer' obligations although now uniting them with 'good service provider' requirements. It has also been understood as the government's effort to 're-establish a new political understanding with organized labour' in the NHS (Stuart and Martínez Lucio, 2000).

The Department of Health took pains to explain that staff involvement (direct employee participation) was being promoted to provide channels for 'employee voice' that were additional to, rather than a substitute for, union-based employee representation in extant joint consultation and negotiation forums. However, it was simultaneously involved in constructing a new, consensus-orientated Social Partnership Forum that enjoined national union leaderships and the NHS employers' representation body in discussion with health ministers about the benefits of partnership working and its contribution to NHS modernisation. The union–management negotiated *Agenda for Change* agreement in 2003–4 included a clause that committed the signatory unions to work in partnership with managements locally, to achieve the principles of the agreement. And the Social Partnership Forum was revamped, most recently in 2007, when a formal partnership agreement was concluded by the Department of Health, national leaderships of the main NHS unions and NHS employers that delineated a three-tier structure of partnership working (union–employer cooperation) at national, regional and local levels (Department of Health, 2007).

Research problems

Writing in 2002, Martínez Lucio and Stuart described partnership in the NHS as a 'bureaucratic and centrally driven approach to organisational change' (253). Our research conducted at around the same time at a large general hospital trust explored some of the critical issues, tensions and potential contradictions of the partnership project.

First, what did staff involvement and partnership working mean at the local level of the NHS employing organisation when the prescription had come from above for this 'style' of working, with prescribed objectives defined in relation to other performance targets? What discretion did local managers have to engage in 'mutuality' and 'reciprocal exchange' (Guest and Peccei, 2001) with employees and their collective representation bodies? Second, how were unions locally responding to the partnership agenda and what implications did it have for union policymaking (i.e. union–member relations)? Industrial relations have been highly centralised in the state sector and in the NHS many 'professional unions' have a short-lived history of workplace union structure (Kessler and Heron, 2001). A stimulus for change was provided by Conservative government efforts in the 1990s to devolve pay determination. That is to say that some commentators (notably Fairbrother, 1996, 2000) espied opportunities for a union renewal based on active membership participation in democratic debate and policy formulation. Yet they were aware that realisation of these opportunities was contingent upon union and workplace union activists' orientation (whether it was membership, management or union facing) and the management response. Management hostility or support could constrain union renewal opportunities, the latter by incorporating union representatives in the management of workplace change that employees experienced as increased surveillance and exhortation to achieve performance targets. Much of the literature critical of the ideology of workplace partnership focuses on the potential for union incorporation in management (e.g. Taylor and Ramsay, 1998), but there are alternative scenarios; for example, a centralisation of union decision-making that distances union leaders from members but with no apparent increase in the former's influence in management or over workplace developments. Third, therefore, and probably the most critical of the issues raised by the partnership agenda, are the forms of staff involvement sponsored, and ways in which these have been experienced by employees: as the opportunity to contribute to organisational decision-making or as exhortation to be committed, adaptable and hard working?

Our research was conducted in 2002 at a large NHS hospital trust (hereafter, General Hospital Trust) located on two main sites in a city in southern England. The Trust had 7500 (full-time equivalent) employees. Women comprised the majority of the workforce and more than 80 per cent of some occupational groups (e.g. nurses). Trade union/ professional association membership overall density was estimated to be around 50 per cent, and to exceed 80 per cent among qualified nursing staff. A formal partnership agreement was concluded between Trust management and senior workplace union and professional association representatives in 2000.

The research used qualitative and quantitative data collection methods to explore employees' views and experiences of the partnership working and staff involvement initiatives. The perspectives of managers, and the interpretations placed on the concept of partnership by lay trade union and professional association representatives (hereafter, trade union representatives), were explored through interviews and the analysis of management and union documents. The research was concentrated within four directorates that together employed the main occupational groups represented in the Trust's workforce.

In total, 68 interviews were recorded with an average duration of one hour. Three interviews were with Trust directors and 17 were with operational directors, line managers and HR advisors attached to the four directorates. Nine senior lay officials from the recognised trade unions and 39 staff were also interviewed. Out of the 1200 question-naires distributed to employees, 452 usable responses were returned, a response rate of 38 per cent. The following discussion of the findings starts with some brief details about the local industrial relations context in which the union–management partnership agreement was con-cluded. The institutions that it established for employees' indirect (or representative) participation in Trust decision-making are sketched, and the pressures bearing on managers of the directorates to develop employee communications and staff involvement are considered. Employees' evaluation of the extent of their direct and indirect par-ticipation in organisational decision-making is then analysed.

The partnership agreement

The Trust was formed at the end of the 1990s through a merger of two others, hereafter denoted as Trust A and Trust B. The hospital services overlapped (for example, both had acute care departments) and Conser-vative government NHS reforms in the 1990s had placed them in competition for the contracts awarded by local purchasing authorities.

> Going back ten or fifteen years, we were in competition with them because the Tories had said well, you know, whoever gets the con-tract you know is going to have the money.
>
> (Biomedical scientist, Trust A)

The task for the management of the merged Trust was to integrate and rationalise services in order to achieve the financial and operational performance improvement objectives of the merger. The managers of clinical directorates became responsible for the services delivered at each of the main hospital sites, and in some departments employees were now required to be location-mobile; that is, to rotate between the two main hospitals on a regular or more ad hoc basis. The Royal College of Nursing (RCN) and UNISON were the largest unions at both trusts. And yet the configuration of union–management relations had developed differently at the two hospitals in the 1990s. The HR managers whom we interviewed presented the contrast as one of adversarial relations at Trust A that stemmed from senior managers' autocratic management style, and the cooperation between unions and management achieved at Trust B where, from its formation, senior managers had sought to involve the unions at 'strategic level', by giving status to the Trust-level joint consultation committee. The committee met regularly and was attended by the Trust's chief executive. A formal agenda of discussion items, agreed by the staff and management sides, was issued in advance; the minutes of meetings were circulated and so on. Other interviewees, however, highlighted other aspects of industrial relations at the two sites. At Trust A, some lay union leaders had achieved some success – measured in terms of union joining and also the ability to challenge management decision-making, at least on some issues – by pursuing an organising approach to union recruitment, and the development of workplace activism. The Manufacturing, Science and Finance union (MSF that was later Amicus and is now UNITE) that organised among scientific and technical staff was the principal example. Senior stewards from each of the main unions recalled that at Trust B, their faith in management had been severely shaken in 1997, when senior managers unilaterally imposed staff car parking charges. It was in the context of threatened industrial action on the issue that senior managers had proposed a formal partnership agreement, to restore cooperative industrial relations. The immediate HR agenda at the time of the merger of the two trusts was to unify the separate bargaining and consultation structures and achieve such harmonisation of employment policies, working practices, grading and 'unsocial hours' payments that would facilitate cross-site working. The larger remit was to achieve the HR and organisational performance targets set by the New Labour government. Senior stewards from the main unions recalled how it had been the unions who were 'the first in the trusts to actually merge into one', and also indicated that the initiative had come from HR.

> We had two HR directors who ... I think, must have seen that was going to be essential, that we should get ourselves organised, and they gave us two days at a conference centre and a facilitator and told us to get on and sort it.

The senior workplace union representatives from all unions at each of the trusts had been invited to meet to agree on a preferred style of working with management, and the cross-site alliances that were forged amassed a majority (not unanimous) vote in favour of a partnership approach. The pro-partnership stewards explained they had felt it was a more mature and less 'macho' approach to the conduct of relations with management than had existed previously (the reference was to Trust A). By the same token, they believed there was scope for joint problem solving with management to progress shared aims or, at least, to resolve differences in ways that were mutually acceptable.

> I personally feel that it is the best way to be. I think if there's a problem I will work with the management to solve it. I don't think there's any point in throwing things as them and banging the table, unless things are falling apart. There will always be a place for banging the table, but banging the table at the beginning doesn't seem to be very good tactics.
>
> ... we can use these now, there are so many tools that we can use and because there is this idea that we can meet and we can sit across the table, I think we do get further along the line.

Moreover, there were 'new tools' – as these union representatives described the new consultation forums instituted with the partnership agreement – that ostensibly inserted a collective employee voice at the level of corporate governance. However, some cynicism had developed by 2002, even among the stewards who were the most enthusiastic for partnership working, as we elaborate later. The formal partnership agreement adopted at the Trust in 2000 prescribed a 'Trust-wide system of employee relations' that would operate at all levels in accordance with TUC (1999) partnership principles, that include open and transparent management (see Chapter 1). It provided for a hierarchy of union–management consultation forums at the 'corporate' level of the Trust, although it left ambiguous the relationship between these. At the base was the Joint Consultation and Negotiation Committee (JCNC) that now covered both sites. It included the members of the newly merged Joint Union Committee (JUC) and, on the management side, the heads of the clinical directorates and of the HR department. It had the remit of providing a forum for 'consultation and dialogue to take place on all organisation-wide and general issues, including the development and implementation of corporate business plans and a forum for the 'negotiation of Agreements on Employment Policies and Procedures'. Above the JCNC was inserted a new Partnership Forum, with a membership that overlapped that of the JCNC, although it also included the Trust's chief executive. It was to be a forum for joint consultation on strategic policymaking. Above the Partnership Forum was the Trust's governing board and the chair of the JUC was now to be an ex officio member.

HR managers thought the innovations were quite radical. A senior member of the department commented that 'the information that we share with our trade unions goes way beyond what other organisations would be ready to share'. However, in common with other members of the department, he discussed staff involvement and partnership working as almost separate projects and the latter as a matter of bringing the unions on board to agree (or legitimise) corporate decisions made by the Trust's management board. This senior manager suggested:

At one level, I think partnership is the concept of every member of staff feeling that they are involved in an operation that is valuable and which values their contribution. So it's really like the John Lewis partnership, every employee has a stake in the future of the organisation. That's one level of partnership. The second level of partnership is the one … with the trade unions which is recognition that the trade unions have a useful contribution to make, that in order to make that contribution they need to be regarded as equals in terms of the sharing of information while always recognising that from a statutory perspective it is the Trust Board that is going to take responsibility. So partnership is about engaging in a mutual understanding and securing the bind of trade unions to the strategic direction of operational management of the Trust. … Because at the end of the day, it is the Trust Board which is answerable to the secretary of state not the trade unions and that's the difference. You can't have a real partnership if the partners aren't equally accountable.

There was considerable ambiguity in the formal partnership agreement with the trade unions as regards the integration between partnership working and staff involvement. Formally it was the partnership forum that was to 'oversee the concept and implementation of staff involvement generally'. However, the agreement also gave authority to management at directorate level to develop 'specific consultative arrangements' in keeping with their needs. And HR managers explained it was their policy to devolve authority to the directorates in order to

give 'management responsibility themselves to manage staff'. Directorates were under the management of a clinician and an operations
director, and were served by an advisor from the central HR department. In accordance with the HR strategy, the operations director
role had been revised to provide greater local autonomy in HR matters,
including staff consultation and communications. Initially there was
considerable unevenness in the volume as well as the type of initiatives
pursued at directorate level. This was in large part because managers
at this level were preoccupied in merging services across the two hospital sites and finding the means of meeting the array of initiatives
and performance targets set by government and, in turn, the Trust's
senior management. Nevertheless, pressures from corporate HR for
middle managers to make staff involvement a priority grew. In 2001–2
the occasion was the run up to the Trust's submission for the HR
Improved Working Lives Practice accreditation. The results of the annual
staff attitude survey – that NHS employing organisations had been
obliged to conduct since April 2000 – would count in the external audit,
and provided considerable stimulus to innovation for some managers.
A poor rating might appear to higher managers as a reflection of poor
management performance at the middle level. The extent of development of novel forms of consultation and communication continued
to vary between directorates that delivered different 'front line' or
support clinical services (acute care and surgery compared to pathology) or employed manual rather than medical and nursing staff.
Nevertheless, there was a discernible trend across directorates towards
a more coordinated use of downwards communication, sometimes
involving team briefing and, in some directorates, use of upwards
problem-solving including staff away days and focus groups.

Partnership in practice? The employees' voice

The theory of workplace partnership is that an appropriate integration
of direct and indirect employee participation can mutually benefit
employees and the employing organisation (Guest and Peccei, 2001;
Boxall and Purcell, 2003). Employees' enhanced voice in organisational
decision-making translates, for the employer, into a more committed, adaptable and productive workforce. The principles have been
reiterated in Department of Health publications and HR 'standards'
and targets (e.g. 1999, 2002, 2003). At our case study hospital trust,

a formal partnership agreement dated from 2000. And yet, among the 39 employees interviewed in our research in the spring and summer of 2002, few knew much about the concept of partnership at work (or partnership working, in NHS parlance). Many of the workplace union representatives interviewed acknowledged that the concept probably 'doesn't resonate much with employees' and argued that they (as representatives) were in part to blame. The problem tended to be framed as a 'failure of communicating the idea of partnership', as one steward expressed the point, rather than inadequate consultation of members and potential members. Yet a senior steward representing manual employees was more blunt and described partnership working at the Trust as a procedural affair at the top of the organisation that was not in any way reflected in managers' receptivity to the employees' voice at lower levels.

> The thing is, partnership has got to mean partnership. It's got to mean partnership from the top to the bottom and I don't mean cosy little meetings between the executive and non-executive directors and a bunch of shop stewards. It means a commitment to partnership in all, the proper dictionary definition, working together, from the top to the bottom. It's not satisfactory just to set up some sort of ad hoc committee and for it not to be cascaded and inspected, if you like, to make sure what happens at the top has got to happen at the bottom … Some of these people, they've got to do as they are bid by the directors, but there is a void, there is a gap.

In fact there was auditing of managers' performance in respect to staff involvement; as suggested, the findings of the annual staff attitude survey counted as evidence in the Trust's submissions for *Improved Working Lives* accreditation. Yet the point remained that managers themselves were not sufficiently empowered to engage in a relationship of mutuality with employees.

Direct employee participation

Direct employee participation – or staff involvement in NHS terminology – includes task participation and management communications that may be one-way (downwards) or two-way (Marchington and Wilkinson, 2000). As regards the first, a majority (58 per cent) of the employees surveyed reported that they were satisfied or very satis-fied with the amount of influence they had over their job. Yet there was substantial variation by occupation; in the pathology directorate, for example, many employees argued that technological change was denuding jobs of intellectual content and only 42 per cent of the scientific and technical staff surveyed reported satisfaction with job influence. And, as indicated in Chapter 2, the Trust alongside CityCo – the other public sector organisation included in our case study research – performed relatively poorly on this measure, in compari-son with the aerospace and financial services case organisations. It is of interest, therefore, that while majorities of surveyed employees (in all occupational groups) at General Hospital Trust felt they had some or a lot of influence in deciding what tasks they had to do and how they carried these out, majorities in most occupational groups (an exception being doctors) indicated that supervisors had influence in these deci-sions and/or that there were written specifications. Many among the nurses who were interviewed highlighted the increase in formal pro-tocols, set by clinical governing bodies beyond the Trust, so that 'there are guidelines for everything really, and there's not much you can do in your own way' (qualified nurse, surgery directorate).

The NHS has been in the throes of reform for the past three decades and there has been substantial change in work organisation and work-ing practices at General Hospital Trust, not least arising from the merger. Managers at all levels were under pressure to achieve the Trust's financial targets, shaped by government policies and priorities for the 'targeted expenditure' flowing from local commissioning author-ities. Staffing shortages were acute in some areas; there was a shortfall in the supply of qualified nurses in some directorates and also diffi-culties in recruiting and retaining clerical and manual ancillary staff. Not surprisingly, our interview and survey data showed that workload increase had been the most notable experience for most employees. Seventy-one per cent of surveyed employees reported that the respon-sibilities in their job had increased over the last three years, and all managers gave this response. Seventy-one per cent of survey respon-dents indicated their experience had been work intensification (an increase in the amount of work they were expected to complete each week). A third (31 per cent) of respondents indicated there had been prolongation of their working week and the proportion rose to 58 per cent among managers (Table 5.1).

Table 5.1 Employees' experience of work intensification and extensification in the past three years, by occupational group

Occupational group	Increase (%)	Decrease (%)	Unchanged (%)
Change to the amount of work I am expected to complete each week			
All respondents	71	3	26
Manager	95	0	5
Doctor	54	7	39
Nurse qualified	81	2	17
Nurse unqualified	64	0	36
Scientific & technical	64	2	34
Admin & clerical	61	0	39
Skilled manual	75	8	17
Other manual	69	5	26
Change to the number of hours I am expected to work each week			
All respondents	31	4	65
Manager	58	0	42
Doctor	44	16	40
Nurse qualified	34	6	60
Nurse unqualified	23	0	77
Scientific & technical	27	2	71
Admin & clerical	32	0	68
Skilled manual	33	0	67
Other manual	14	3	83

Note: n = 452.

It was in this context that managers – of directorates or wards or departments within them – had been urged to make staff involvement and partnership working a priority, alongside other HR targets (flexible working and work-life balance), financial and patient service targets (reduced patient waiting times, improvement in patient environment). In practice, a large volume of information flowed from the Trust's corporate centre to middle managers, ward and departmental managers about national policy, national standards in clinical governance, the Trust's financial performance, its expenditure savings priorities and so on. Indeed, middle managers reported it was an exhausting task simply to wade through the avalanche of information and select what appeared to be the most pressing items for dissemination to staff.

> How do we get the communications across, bearing in mind the amount of paperwork that comes on a day-to-day basis? I could build walls with it. It's just ridiculous. You have to filter through what's relevant and what isn't and the timescales.
>
> (Senior Nurse)

In addition, corporate managers and the HR department were making assiduous efforts to make information about Trust policies and procedures, central government policy initiatives and the initiatives launched locally in response openly available to staff on the intranet, and to highlight particular items in the Trust's monthly magazine. The view among a number of employee interviewees was again that there was a large amount of information but that it could be difficult to make sense of any of it.

> We are probably given more information ... I think I have noticed there's probably a policy of making sure everybody knows things. But sometimes you think well, so what, it doesn't actually tell me anything.
>
> (Biomedical Scientist)

At the level of the separate directorates there had been a range of staff involvement initiatives. In the surgery directorate, where nurses were the largest occupational group, the initiatives included upward problem solving – in the form of manager and staff away days and focus groups – in addition to team-briefings and a newly instituted directorate newsletter.

However, our questionnaire survey of employees in four directorates suggested there was a substantial 'staff involvement gap' (Table 5.2). Only 37 per cent of respondents thought managers were good, or very good, at involving employees in decision-making. Roughly equal proportions of survey respondents thought managers were good, and poor, at keeping everyone up to date about changes at work (49 per cent and 47 per cent respectively). But the majority view was that managers were poor or very poor at providing everyone with a chance to comment on proposed changes (54 per cent) and at responding to suggestions from employees (54 per cent).

Managers were the most likely to rate managerial performance as good or very good on each of these activities, although they were little

Table 5.2 Employees' evaluation of managers' performance in respect to employee communications and involvement, by occupation group

Occupational group	Very good (%)	Good (%)	Poor (%)	Very poor (%)	Undecided (%)
Involving employees in decision-making					
All respondents	8	29	41	15	7
Manager	11	47	26	5	11
Doctor	0	23	49	14	14
Nurse qualified	12	37	34	13	4
Nurse unqualified	6	31	34	23	6
Scientific & technical	3	22	52	12	11
Admin & clerical	13	28	46	8	5
Skilled manual	14	36	29	21	0
Other manual	9	20	42	22	7
Keeping everyone up to date with proposed changes					
All respondents	9	40	34	13	4
Manager	0	74	16	10	0
Doctor	0	28	44	19	9
Nurse qualified	15	43	30	11	1
Nurse unqualified	9	40	31	17	3
Scientific & technical	5	43	34	10	8
Admin & clerical	13	33	38	13	3
Skilled manual	8	54	23	8	7
Other manual	8	33	38	18	3
Providing employees with the chance to comment on proposed changes					
All respondents	6	35	40	15	4
Manager	5	63	21	11	0
Doctor	0	23	47	21	9
Nurse qualified	10	32	43	12	3
Nurse unqualified	3	51	26	20	0
Scientific & technical	1	39	44	8	8
Admin & clerical	8	35	39	10	8
Skilled manual	7	50	29	7	7
Other manual	4	28	40	25	3
Responding to suggestions from employees					
All respondents	5	32	40	13	10
Manager	0	47	32	11	10
Doctor	0	19	44	16	21
Nurse qualified	8	40	37	9	6

(Continued)

Table 5.2   (Continued)

Occupational group	Very good (%)	Good (%)	Poor (%)	Very poor (%)	Undecided (%)
Nurse unqualified	6	29	32	21	12
Scientific & technical	0	33	49	8	10
Admin & clerical	10	26	46	8	10
Skilled manual	7	36	50	0	7
Other manual	5	24	33	28	10

Note: n = 452.

more convinced than other occupational groups about their prowess in responding to employees' suggestions. Nurses were more positive about managers' performance than other non-managerial staff. But it was only on the issue of keeping everyone up to date on proposed changes that a majority in this occupational group rated managers' performance as good or very good. The employee interviews suggested a range of factors that contributed to the staff involvement deficit. For example, in surgery, where use of upward problem-solving techniques was relatively more developed than in the four other directorates our research focused on, some employees noted it took courage for individuals to articulate views in the 'public forum' of the focus group, with senior managers present.

> there are focus group meetings. So they can tell us things and we can say, if we dare ... We can say our concerns and it may be just a case sometimes that they say why this is, what's going on, what's happened.
>
> (Nurse, qualified, junior grade)

Others thought that while the focus groups provided an opportunity for staff to raise issues, the churn in the participants (shift rotas prevented many staff from attending regularly) meant that issues raised tended to 'get lost somewhere along the system' (ward receptionist). In the pathology department, within the clinical support directorate, it was the workplace union that supplied a main pressure for managers to engage in information sharing, but at one hospital site (Trust B) there were few union representatives. In the facilities directorate, the porters, cleaning and catering staff complained that senior managers frequently cancelled scheduled 'team briefings'. This was sometimes to firefight service delivery problems arising from staff shortages and sometimes to attend to pressing corporate matters. In any event, the impression given to the staff was that their voice was not an especially high priority for senior managers within the directorate (or that it was a voice that managers did not want to hear).

Yet it was the interviews with directorate managers that provided the critical insight. Their interpretation of staff involvement appeared to be employee consultation on local management plans that had been approved by the Trust's corporate board. In surgery, for example, the major initiative that was about to be unfurled was the split of elective and trauma patient care, as between the two main hospital sites (so that each would become a dedicated facility for one or other of the two 'specialisms'). This had large implications for staff in terms of workloads, skills, continuing professional development and quality of working life. The directorate's managers had sought the approval of Trust senior managers before they felt it safe to 'involve more people in consultation'. A reason was that the restructuring would require financial expenditure and a case had to be proved to corporate managers that the expenditure would pay-off in terms of contribution to financial and operational performance improvement targets. Overlaying this, however, was what a number of interviewees – employees, workplace union representatives and managers – referred to as the 'climate of fear' that appeared to hang on middle and more senior managers. The requirement was to 'hit' prescribed performance targets and the safest bet (in terms of job security) was to ensure that any innovation had been given the corporate approval seal.

Indirect employee participation

The Partnership Agreement in principle afforded employees indirect participation in consultation forums with senior management that addressed strategic policy matters as well as HR and employment issues. The JCNC was the longest established of these forums although, of course, it had existed before the merger as separate committees (dominated by contrasting 'styles' of union-management relations) at the two hospitals. Among the employees we surveyed in 2002, however, only 19 per cent indicated they were aware of the JCNC and only

10 per cent claimed to know who represented them in this forum. Not surprisingly, few employees were certain their views were represented at the JCNC; 47 per cent reported they were not and 48 per cent suggested they did not know. Senior stewards had devoted much time and energy to the JCNC and emphasised the large effort they made to publicise its work; minutes of meetings were available to staff on the intra-net and there was a regular column in the Trust's magazine. Hence, among their explanations for its apparent lack of visibility was employee apathy. An alternative interpretation, articulated by some workplace union representatives, was that it was the content of JCNC proceedings that was the problem together with its limited achievement in progressing issues that were of staff concern. As one steward, representing manual workers in the facilities directorate summarised:

> They start talking about all these highfalutin things, and they can't even get the blokes' pay right.

The JCNC agenda was dominated by the concerns of the HR department, which were to achieve harmonisation of policies and procedures in the wake of the merger, and to ensure relevant evidence was in place for the Trust to succeed in Department of Health HR audits. Some of the issues were relatively uncontroversial so that consensus was easy to achieve. However, other issues were difficult to agree upon because they challenged the Trust's expenditure priorities. These included the harmonisation of manual workers' bonus pay, which lingered as an unresolved agenda item over many months. At the time of our research, there was some cynicism among workplace union representatives about management's commitment to partnership working. This was even among the stewards who had been the most enthusiastic for the partnership agreement. A particular grievance was that the Partnership Forum had met infrequently. The former chief executive had left and the new job-holder prioritised other matters, such as financial targets (that the Trust currently was unable to achieve). Senior stewards for the most part remained committed to the project of partnership but were now more inclined to see senior management's commitment as tokenistic. They argued that if senior managers were interested in partnership it was because 'they've been told to be'; that is, managers had been obliged to set in place relevant arrangements in order to tick-off yet another in the long list of targets set centrally, by government.

> I think they might pretend to get involved with it because it's like *Improved Working Lives*, they're all things that have come down centrally and it's 'to get your staff, to get your money, to get your independence' you have to be seen, or try and provide evidence that you are doing these things that the government requires you to do. Whether they really believe that it is a good way to work, I don't know.
>
> We have to keep bringing them up and asking managers what a definition of working in partnership means to them. So I think it was more a paper exercise really, but it seems to be tailing off a bit now and we're back into our finding things out and saying 'what's going on here?' and 'why has this been?'.

Workplace union representatives questioned management's attachment to partnership, and our research found that among the Trust's employees few perceived any shift towards a new relationship of mutuality. For example, a (slim) majority of surveyed employees (54 per cent) agreed or strongly agreed with the proposition that 'good relations exist between management and employees' (Table 5.3) and the 'positive' response owed partly to the inclusion of managers (who were more inclined than most occupational groups to agree with the proposition). With the exception of managers, survey respondents were doubtful that 'good relations exist between management and unions'; only 27 per cent of the total agreed or strongly agreed with the proposition. Most respondents (78 per cent) agreed with the principle that 'management and employees should be members of the same team'. Yet two-thirds (64 per cent) agreed or strongly agreed that management here 'believe they are in a separate team to employees' (and managers were as inclined to this evaluation as other occupational staff groups).

Union representation

Union density was estimated to be around 50 per cent at the Trust in 2002, rising to above 80 per cent among some professional occupational groups. Among the employees we surveyed, over 70 per cent who

Table 5.3 Employees' evaluation of the state of employee relations, by occupational group

	Strongly agree (%)	Agree (%)	Disagree (%)	Strongly disagree (%)	Undecided (%)
Good relations exist between management and employees					
All respondents	3	51	25	8	13
Manager	5	79	16	0	0
Doctor	0	29	41	7	23
Nurse qualified	4	58	23	7	8
Nurse unqualified	3	45	20	9	23
Scientific & technical	1	47	26	7	19
Admin & clerical	8	52	24	0	16
Skilled manual	0	71	29	0	0
Other manual	4	47	21	18	10
Good relations exist between management and unions					
All respondents	0	27	17	4	52
Manager	0	84	11	0	5
Doctor	0	18	18	5	59
Nurse qualified	0	31	16	4	49
Nurse unqualified	0	14	14	3	69
Scientific & technical	0	24	18	4	54
Admin & clerical	0	21	16	0	63
Skilled manual	0	29	28	0	43
Other manual	1	21	19	8	51
Management and employees should be members of the same team					
All respondents	19	59	3	2	17
Manager	32	63	5	0	0
Doctor	9	50	12	2	27
Nurse qualified	20	63	2	0	15
Nurse unqualified	17	54	6	0	23
Scientific & technical	24	53	1	1	21
Admin & clerical	13	69	3	3	12
Skilled manual	21	57	7	0	15
Other manual	17	61	0	5	17
Management believe they are in a separate team to employees					
All respondents	21	43	14	2	20
Manager	16	47	37	0	0
Doctor	14	43	21	2	20
Nurse qualified	17	51	11	1	20

(Continued)

Table 5.3   (Continued)

	Strongly agree (%)	Agree (%)	Disagree (%)	Strongly disagree (%)	Undecided (%)
Nurse unqualified	23	41	3	3	29
Scientific & technical	12	42	17	4	25
Admin & clerical	23	39	15	0	23
Skilled manual	14	50	22	0	14
Other manual	41	32	12	1	14

Note: n = 452.

were doctors, nurses or managers indicated they were union/professional association members while 'union density' fell to 24 per cent among administrative and clerical staff. Union membership may be valued for the professional or occupational services derived. Yet, among our surveyed employees, although most obviously among those who were union members, it was evident there was also substantial demand for traditional union services.

Asked who they thought, ideally, would best represent them to gain a pay increase, 57 per cent of all employee respondents and 72 per cent of union members among them selected trade union representation among the options included in the survey question (see Table 5.4). Fifty-one per cent of all surveyed employees and 70 per cent of union members among them thought union representation their best bet if they were being disciplined by management.

The survey and interview data also made it clear that for many employees – union members and potential members – union representatives were not very visible in the workplace. A third of all survey respondents (35 per cent) reported they never had contact with union representatives about workplace matters and a third (34 per cent) indicated they did not know who the union representatives were. However, there was variation by occupational group (and hence by union); for example, a majority of the scientific and technical staff surveyed (58 per cent) suggested they had frequent or occasional contact with union representatives about workplace matters whereas the proportion fell to a fifth (21 per cent) among nurses. Of course, the different unions had different histories of workplace organising and stewards' 'constituencies' varied in size; the RCN, for example, had a few workplace representatives 'servicing' a large membership

Table 5.4   Union and non-union members' views of who best represents them in dealing with management about different workplace issues

	Myself (%)	Trade union (%)	Another employee (%)	Someone else (%)
If I want to gain a pay increase				
All respondents	30	57	3	10
Current union member	19	72	2	7
Past union member	40	48	2	10
Never a member	50	28	5	17
If I have a work-related problem or grievance				
All respondents	45	37	12	6
Current union member	34	51	12	3
Past union member	61	19	7	13
Never a member	63	14	13	10
If a manager wanted to discipline me				
All respondents	33	51	8	8
Current union member	22	70	4	4
Past union member	45	32	16	7
Never a member	51	17	13	19

population, although this would appear to be typical of the case at other NHS trusts (Kessler and Heron, 2001, p. 378). Senior stewards had 'time off' facilities for union work but other representatives undertook the role in addition to their normal workload. The point, however, is that the tasks of servicing the central partnership institutions absorbed a good deal of the unions' already stretched resources. A senior steward described how his role had become more corporate-focused:

> The corporate sort of representation has increased, especially since the merger of the trusts. I am taking on more responsibility in helping the staff side with issues, representing the whole of the workforce and not just my members. So I do get involved more heavily, for example, sitting on steering groups and on committees.

And since there were relatively few workplace representatives, he did not have the time to engage in recruitment and left membership communications largely to the regional office.

The central partnership forum of the JCNC did not appear to be very visible to many employees, for reasons discussed. Thus, rather than perceiving union representatives as having become incorporated in management, the view of many employees seemed to be that the unions achieved marginal influence in management decision-making. Two-fifths of surveyed employees (39 per cent) agreed or strongly agreed with the proposition that 'unions here take notice of members' problems and complaints'. The proportion was nearer half (48 per cent) among union members and higher among some of the unions present in the workplace (70 per cent in the case of Amicus members). However, only 28 per cent of all survey respondents agreed or strongly agreed that 'unions here are taken seriously by management' and the proportion was a little higher – 31 per cent – among employees who were union members. Only a fifth (21 per cent) of surveyed employees and a quarter (24 per cent) of those who were union members agreed or strongly agreed that 'unions make a difference to what it is like to work here'.

Conclusion

Partnership in the NHS has been described as a 'bureaucratic and centrally driven approach to organisational change' (Martínez Lucio and Stuart, 2002, p. 253). Performance management targets and considerable volumes of literature have been supplied to encourage NHS employers and their management staff to establish partnership working and staff involvement 'on the ground'. This is within the context of the larger programme of NHS 'modernisation' that has included reforms of pay and grading and of work organisation in pursuit of higher performance from NHS service provider organisations and staff. Echoing the wider management literature on partnership at work, Department of Health publications propose that staff involvement and partnership working achieves positive outcomes for employees, the employing organisation and users of NHS services. Our research at one NHS hospital trust in 2002 focused on the experiences of employees. The Trust's managers had put in place a number of the prescribed partnership practices, albeit unevenly, between directorates and among different occupational groups. Yet our interview and employee survey data suggested that employees were largely unconvinced that they had involvement in organisational decision-making, either directly or via their representatives. Indeed, few employees appeared to be aware of the central partnership forum, the JCNC. The main experience reported by employees was increased workload. A number of factors contributed to the worker participation deficit. The most obvious among these were the conditions governing management decision-making and, critically, the performance management regime of central government. The pressures on managers to achieve the array of performance targets – including financial targets and faster patient 'throughput' – limited their discretion and, in turn, their capacity to 'empower' employees. Indeed, workplace union representatives who had been pro-partnership in 2000 were in 2002 cynical that senior management's commitment to partnership working was any deeper than the need to demonstrate compliance with Department of Health HR targets. Managers of the different directorates were under pressure to achieve the performance improvements demanded by the Trust's board of directors and tended to understand staff involvement targets among these as consultation on decisions that had been reached. The HR department did have a local agenda for courting partnership with the unions that was overlaid by the national agenda. Managers needed to achieve the harmonisation of HR policies and procedures across the two main hospital sites and it was this agenda that largely dominated in the JCNC. Since the issues were remote from the issues that were of concern for employees – including pay and workloads – there was limited incentive to be interested in JCNC affairs. Union representatives' commitment to partnership working with management at trust level served to centralise union decision-making and resources, and to make unions remote from their members. Yet there was unevenness in this respect. Some among the professional unions, with the least history of workplace organising, appeared to be most distanced from those they represented at the Trust while there were stewards within some of the TUC affiliated unions who kept active in union building from the bottom upwards.

Our research was conducted at one hospital trust. Yet similar findings have been made in other studies of staff involvement in the NHS. For example, Bach's (2004) research at three hospital trusts, like ours, found a democratic deficit in the workplace that arose largely from the performance management regime. Of course, change is a more or less continuous obligation for NHS managers and staff. Our study is obviously limited in the extent to which it pre-dates the innovation of NHS foundation trusts that are reported to be 'free from central government control and ... no longer performance managed by health authorities' (Department of Health, 2005). Yet foundation trusts are still subject to performance ratings and systems of inspection. They have new financial freedoms, yet in common with other NHS trusts they operate in an increasingly market environment in which service provider organisations compete for the money that follows the patient. The scope for a substantial injection of democracy at work may remain restricted.

6

Goodbye Blue Sky: Partnership in the UK Aerospace Sector

This chapter presents two case studies of workplace partnership in the aerospace industry, a key strategic sector for Britain's manufacturing base. We first provide a brief account of organisational context by describing recent politico-economic changes affecting the sector along with the distinctive patterns of organisational restructuring that have transformed many UK aerospace plants into 'new flexible firms'. We then provide detailed case study accounts of the impact of restructuring, focusing upon the labour process and patterns of management control. These changes generated widespread feelings of insecurity, grievance and discontent on the shop floor and in the engineering offices. But they did not take hold in an industrial relations vacuum. The chapter analyses two contrasting examples of management attempts to legitimise organisational change by developing partnership relationships with workplace unions. The first is an example of 'informal partnership' characterised by an emphasis upon informality and process. The second is an example of 'formal partnership' governed by written agreement and emphasising process but also a more systematic, methodical approach to recasting management–union relations. In both cases the analysis highlights tensions and contradictions inherent in partnership strategies by drawing on the first hand accounts of union stewards and workers.

The aerospace industry remains the premier sector in UK manufacturing and the largest in global aerospace outside the USA. In 2006, it had a turnover of over £19 billion and employed some 276,000 workers. Of these, 124,000 were employed directly by aircraft, engine and equipment assemblers with the remainder located in supply chains and subcontractors. The industry is also notable for being a prime employer of skilled engineering labour. In 2006, of those employed directly by the aerospace assemblers, 34 per cent were graduate engineers and managers and 31 per cent were technicians, the latter including a large number of skilled production workers (SBAC, 2007). Thus, compared to the rationalised work systems of standardised mass production, the aerospace industry is noteworthy for being a site of high value added engineering with high skill utilisation and technological innovation.

Historically, the sector has also been notable for the strength of its craft-based trade unionism and of recurring patterns of labour militancy, particularly wages militancy (see Danford et al., 2005, pp. 21–36; also Croucher, 1982 and Smith, 1987). More recently, however, leading aerospace companies have been associated with the promotion of the UK's workplace partnership agenda, most conspicuously the sector's largest players, BAe Systems and Airbus UK (TUC, 2000; TUC Partnership Institute, 2000). Indeed, at a time when interest in partnership was at its peak, the results of a human resource strategy survey of managers at 350 UK aerospace assembler and supplier companies did seem to reflect 'mutual gain' partnership rhetoric. The survey found that large majorities of managers claimed to emphasise such strategies as 'raising employee skills', 'encouraging innovation' and 'empowerment'. This compared to less than 10 per cent who prioritised labour rationalisation (SBAC, 2000). In fact, this rhetoric obscured the fact that in recent years record levels of profits and a near trebling of productivity per employee (SBAC, 2007) were actually based on the systematic stripping out of labour from the design and production process. During the last decade, the UK industry lost a quarter of its workforce as a result of recurrent mass redundancies at many plants throughout the UK.

The high level of job losses was partly due to short-term effects, such as cyclical recession in civil aerospace markets (exacerbated by an initial post-September 11, 2001 downturn). The intensification of global competition between suppliers in Europe, North and South America, China and the Far East has been another ingredient. However, a more consistent longer-term factor for labour deployment has been the impact of company and workplace restructuring. The advent of the New Right in the 1980s – and associated neoliberal economic policy – provided the initial catalyst for change. Major players, such as British Aerospace and Rolls-Royce were privatised in this period. At the same time, Thatcher's Conservative government imposed new competitive tendering policies on the industry to replace 'cost-plus' defence contracts. This, in combination with post-Cold War cuts in national defence budgets and recession in civil aerospace markets engendered a major squeeze on labour as firms maintained profitability by slashing labour costs and closing down plants. Since that time, and in the politico-economic environment of New Labour's neoliberalism, the structure of the aerospace industry has undergone a process of further internationalisation and capital concentration as different capitals have reacted to spiralling product development costs by forming new international corporate networks, joint programme initiatives, joint ventures, strategic alliances and sometimes full mergers mostly in Europe and the USA.

This new, complex landscape of capital concentration in the industry is represented diagrammatically in Figure 6.1 (it excludes aero-engines). The new alliances and shifting patterns of ownership exemplify the emergence of new organisational forms, with 'blurred boundaries' as described by writers in the field of organisational studies (see, for example, Barley and Kunda, 2004, pp. 303–4). The changes have potential implications for labour deployment and costs in that duplicated resources may become subject to rationalisation. At the same time as these company structures have radically changed, individual workplaces have also been subject to major redesign and restructuring. Using Ackroyd and Procter's (1998) concept of the 'new flexible firm', we have described previously the reconfiguration of aerospace workplaces into more fragmented and flexible business units (see Danford et al., 2005 and 2003). Driven by new systems of financial control, labour deployment has become marked by a shift away from skill demarcation based on specialised production and design functions. Labour utilisation in the new flexible firm has come to be based on increasing task and numerical flexibility through the use of profit centres, project matrix systems, production cells and core-periphery employment systems (incorporating the more widespread use of subcontract labour, agency labour, temporary labour and outsourcing).

The chapter explores a number of critical questions governing the nature of organisational change under so-called high-performance work regimes. Our key line of enquiry concerns the impact of change on worker interests. For example, what is the impact of restructuring

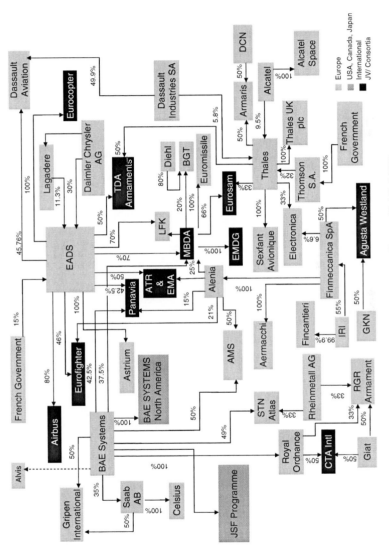

Figure 6.1 Major European aerospace and defence cross-holdings (*Source:* SBAC, 2003).

and new systems of management control on employee autonomy and involvement at work? To what extent does management's partnership agenda actually succeed in its objective of legitimising change? Comparing different forms of partnership, how do workers and unions perceive management attempts to recast the conventions of plant-based industrial relations? And to what extent does partnership actually deliver on its 'mutual gains' agenda, for example, in terms of union influence, employee voice and employment security?

Airframes and JetCo

The two case studies are large, UK-based design and production aerospace plants. They are located in the south of England, one in a rural community, the other in an urban setting. The plants are given the pseudonyms 'Airframes' and 'JetCo'.

Airframes was responsible for the design and assembly of a particular generic type of aircraft that can be used for both civil and military purposes. The factory employed just over 4000 workers comprising approximately 600 managers and supervisors, 1500 production workers (90 per cent of whom were skilled) and 1900 technical and administrative staff. The JetCo factory was responsible for the design and production of aero-engines. It employed 4300 workers, comprising 1800 production workers (80 per cent skilled) and 2500 managers, technical and administrative staff. Both plants employed high proportions of engineering and commercial graduates (or equivalents such as those qualified to HND/HNC level).

There were two main trade union bargaining groups in each plant and all four of these were dominated by the AMICUS trade union (now merged with the T&GWU to form UNITE). On each shop floor, the majority of skilled production workers were represented by AMICUS-AEEU with the remaining semi-skilled groups represented mostly by the T&GWU. These joined to form single manual bargaining groups. In the white-collar areas technical staff were represented by AMICUS-MSF while a much smaller group of administrative staff were members of ACTSS at Airframes and APEX at JetCo. In both cases these members joined to form single non-manual bargaining groups. Manual union membership density at both plants was virtually 100 per cent, while non-manual densities for AMICUS-MSF were around 80 per cent but lower for the clerical unions.

At both plants the architecture for collective bargaining and consultation comprised regular joint management–union negotiating sessions over pay and conditions of employment, plus different consultation forums for discussing broader strategic issues. At Airframes, the latter comprised a plant-based company council along with a multisite UK works council; and at JetCo, a transnational works council (covering plants in the UK, Germany and North America) along with a multisite UK Information and Consultation Council introduced in 2005, in compliance with the New Labour Government's Information and Consultation of Employees Regulations. The different councils brought together managers and senior stewards to discuss such issues as corporate strategy, future projects and staffing levels.

The bulk of the data were collected during 2001 and 2002 with a small number of additional interviews completed in 2005–6. During 2001–2 we carried out taped interviews with 142 staff divided more or less equally between the two plants. These comprised 28 senior and line managers, 24 union representatives, 41 production workers (nearly all of whom were skilled) and 49 non-manual employees (comprising graduate engineers, technical workers and administrative staff). In addition, a questionnaire survey collected 878 responses from a sample of 1100 manual and non-manual employees at Airframes (an 80 per cent response rate) and 604 responses from a sample of 974 employees at JetCo (62 per cent). The response rate at Airframes was notably high. The prime reason for this was that senior management gave workers time off to fill in the questionnaires at specially organized team briefing sessions.

Restructuring and financial control: The case of Airframes

Airframes began life as an oil engine manufacturer at the turn of the last century, and then developed aircraft production during the century's two world wars. The company eventually became a leading global manufacturer. During the last two decades, its corporate structure changed radically as the processes of capital concentration and consolidation in the sector took hold. In the mid-1980s, a joint venture was formed with a leading USA aerospace multinational; in 1994, the company was subject to a hostile takeover by one of the UK's largest engineering multinationals; and in 2004, the company completed a second, international merger with an Italian civil aircraft manufacturer. The merger created a new division of 10,000 workers. The case study factory was the company's largest UK operation.

One of the most significant organizational changes to affect management control on the shop floor was implemented in the late 1990s. The factory had already been broken up into three different business units: assembly, transmissions and structures. The largest of these was responsible for airframe assembly and was the location of most of the research reported here. On the shop floor, managers attempted to secure more efficient labour utilisation and greater transparency in labour costs by introducing lean manufacturing techniques such as teamworking, continuous improvement groups and just in time. The design and assembly process underwent further fragmentation when the airframe business unit was reorganised into a basic matrix structure similar to organisational forms pioneered in the USA aerospace industry (Allen, 1986; Katz and Allen, 1985). This comprised different product and process program directorates along with a separate matrix for R&D and design engineering. The effect on labour control was to allow greater flexibility by incorporating multiple project working and task enlargement into the labour process. This was summarised by the plant's engineering director:

> And that really meant that for a large percentage of the people their day-to-day responsibilities would change somewhat. Their particular discipline or the act that they would perform would have broadened. So instead of having a traditional design man who passed his work to a traditional stress man they've now been, to a degree, multi-skilled. So the stressman helps with the upfront design, and on a range of projects rather than a single one.
>
> (Engineering Director)

The changes also generated considerable labour savings and time efficiencies by providing greater transparency of the marginal costs and benefits of different design and production processes. Once the structure was put into place, new more 'entrepreneurial' managers were put in charge of the different programmes and held accountable for stripping out human and material 'waste' from the design-to-manufacturing process. One production director who had put in 25 years' service with the company explained how, over this time, his responsibility had changed. Prior to the reorganisation, emphasis was placed on

coordinating the required labour and material resources to meet production quotas and the demands of complex engineering problems,
irrespective of cost. More recently, however, he had adopted the
mindset and discourse of the cost accountant:

> In terms of productivity, each aircraft has got an allotted number
> of hours per assembly stage. So we measure lead-time from start to
> finish, which you're continually reducing. We measure cost, we
> measure hours to achieve, one hour's earned value in effect. And
> then we're into our five production stages. We measure utilisation,
> which is booked by number, check they're not fucking you about
> that way ... third value analysis, that leads to a productivity analysis
> because actual hours versus budgeted hours gives you productivity,
> and then we use lots of extrapolations for 'are we really achieving
> ops and achieving our value' ... Every Wednesday morning we have
> a shagathon. I get a copy of the data, all the cell managers get a
> copy of the data and we start at one cell and we go on through. I just
> get up and I say the week looked like this boys, you did this right,
> you did that right, you did this bloody wrongly.

What were the reactions of workers in the design and production
areas to these organisational changes? In various ways, our interviews
and questionnaire data highlighted employee resentment and frustration over perceived increases in the level of surveillance and management control. On the shop floor, workers articulated variously
a sense of being treated as a 'number', as a 'child' and as someone who
is subject to constant surveillance. Some examples:

> Airframes was once a caring, sharing company. But over the last
> few years it has plummeted to dark depths. No longer is the
> employee a person but instead we're just a number.
>
> (Aircraft Fitter)

> There is never any give and take in this workplace. We are dictated
> to all the time which in turn makes morale very low.
>
> (Aircraft Fitter)

> The management now focus more on their targets and making
> money, than on the workforce and the final product. As a workforce

we are more flexible now than ever. But we are still treated like children and on a need to know basis.

(Quality Inspector)

[Has the work intensified?] Yes, yes definitely, absolutely. Not so much on break times, break times they only pick on you when it gets quiet. If there's a quiet time then they start poking at you and prodding you with a stick all the time ... I certainly know that when I first started here if somebody came and told you that you had to have this job done by this time then you'd be like, "well the job will be done when it's done and it's as simple as that". I would say, "if you need it then I'll work faster but don't be telling me how long it's going to take me". Whereas on this line now, they say to you this is how many hours you've got on this job, not that you have to specifically work to those but what it means is that they can gauge you.

(Aircraft Fitter)

In the engineering offices, many workers voiced a similar sense of frustration governing the impact on their roles of the new matrix-based flexibility practices. Equally, in the context of the ascendance of accounting and finance and its systems of financial control, they described a sense of decline in engineering values and of the role of the engineer:

Certainly my area, because you talk about people's careers here, I have chosen to make a career with flight testing and they're talking about shifting people to Customer Support. Why would I want to go to customer support? I chose a career over here, not customer support. Okay, it's a job, but you're talking about people's careers. They may as well send us out to McDonalds or something. I think some people are looking at it as, "it's a job so don't moan", but you're looking at people's careers.

(Flight Test Engineer)

What I saw in the last project I did ... There were only half a dozen people I could think of that were consistently in the same position all the way through the programme out of the couple of hundred engineers that I work with. Did that cause resentment? It was frustration more than anything. We've got somebody who would be doing a job, then they had to break off away and then somebody else had to pick it up and you'd be back to square one and it was just bloody frustrating. And it causes stress. Frustration is endemic to stress.

(Principal Engineer)

The thing about Airframes when I first joined I was impressed about how engineering orientated it was. It was basically an engineering company, testosterone-type environment and you got on and did the job and you did the right thing for the right reasons, finding a good engineers' solution to an engineering problem. Now it's basically run by a bunch of pure credit accountants. You're just never allowed to be an engineer, in fact, being an engineer is a dirty word.

(Quality Engineer)

The questionnaire survey results reflected this rank and file experience (see Danford et al., 2005 for a more comprehensive presentation of data). For example, significant proportions of workers indicated that effort rates had intensified during the three years leading up to the research: around half of manual and non-manual workers felt that the amount of work they were expected to complete each week had increased and between two-thirds and three-quarters felt that the degree of flexibility required in their work had increased. Also, two-thirds of manual workers either disagreed or strongly disagreed with the proposition that their job was secure at Airframes. Many workers also indicated the presence of low trust in management-employee relationships and a lack of managerial commitment to the principles of 'employee voice'. For example, when asked whether they believed that management and employees should be members of the same team, very large majorities of manual and non-manual workers felt that this should be the case. But over three-quarters also felt that their management believed they were in a separate team to their employees. And despite a new managerial rhetoric of the need for employee involvement in the 'high performance workplace', two-thirds of Airframes workers felt that they were hardly ever or never consulted on future company plans and four-fifths indicated the same over the question of staffing issues and redundancies.

Restructuring and financial control: The case of JetCo

JetCo is one of the world's leading aero-engine manufacturers. At the beginning of 2005, the company's annual sales stood at £6 billion and it employed a global workforce of 35,000 people. Forty per cent of these workers were employed outside of the UK, for example, in manufacturing locations in 20 different countries. The case study plant was the company's second largest and housed the headquarters for military engines.

In 1998, three years before the research commenced, the plant underwent a programme of organizational restructuring and divisional fragmentation, that, in many respects, was more far-reaching than the Airframes case. Previously a unitary division responsible solely for the design and manufacture of military engines, it was reconfigured into a complex multi-profit centre factory. The company itself was re-organized into a new structure comprising a variety of 'customer focused business units'. Each of these units reported directly to a corporate headquarters. Six units were responsible for different aero-engine markets, the remainder covered other business, such as, power generation, and different support operations. To varying degrees, all customer-facing units were represented on the site. A matrix was formed by introducing a further nine business units responsible for supplying the customer-facing units with the core sub-assemblies of aero-engine construction. For example, combustion systems and turbines. A factory that was previously home to a unitary division was transformed into a location for a plethora of separate businesses, some located in a complex supply chain, others responsible for engine assembly for global markets. In addition, JetCo managers employed industrial consultants armed with the full range of business school jargon, such as 're-engineering' and 'value stream mapping', to reconfigure machinery and labour deployment on the shop floor. Many workers became subject to new patterns of multitasking in teams, and, Japanese style, were expected to participate in kaizen continuous improvement groups aimed ultimately at ratcheting up effort rates.

As we saw at Airframes, management's objective was to secure improved financial control over every aspect of the business, albeit under the guise of 'team/unit decentralization'. The change programmes at JetCo did differ in one notable respect, however. The process of converting UK manufacturing into an assembly operation has come to be known as 'systems integration' (another business school euphemism). Essentially, this involves outsourcing the manufacture of large parts and assemblies to different firms in the supply chain and then acting as final assembler of these parts and providing post-sale services. It is now a common factor of production control in the aerospace sector (Braddon, 2000; Dunne and Macdonald, 2001). The JetCo plant underwent profound change as a result of this labour cost-cutting strategy. By 2001, 65 per cent of the plant's manufacturing processes were outsourced. The objective was to increase this to 80 per cent of the total manufacturing requirement. Outsourcing has been driven by a combination of economic and political factors embodied in the management strategy of 'make-buy'. Make-buy requires managers to cut labour costs by separating out manufacturing operations that could potentially be performed by suppliers offering cheaper labour from those operations requiring highly specialist skills and technologies. The process also has a geopolitical dimension. Aerospace firms attempting to win export orders in highly competitive global markets often resort to establishing joint ventures, licensed overseas production and 'offset' deals with client firms and states. This has inevitable implications for the transfer of jobs away from the major aerospace centres in the USA and UK (Almeida, 2001; Bluestone et al., 1981; Danford et al., 2005; House of Commons Trade and Industry Committee, 2005; Murman et al., 2002). This development has been assisted partly by the relative weakness of organised labour on the shop floor. The general decline in trade union influence in UK manufacturing has contributed to a dilution, in some cases, of workplace-level agreements that previously served to police the use of subcontractors in the aerospace sector (Danford et al., 2003).

JetCo's Operations Director explained the logic of make-buy:

> [Make-buy] determines strategy if you like, you know, what should we make, what should we buy. And we cannot afford to invest in everything and become world class, the world's best in everything. So we are saying we need to determine what we wish to excel in and what we already excel in and concentrate our efforts on that. And if there are other sources outside that can make products cheaper and better than we can, then they ought to get on with that and allow us to concentrate on our strategically important parts and products. What it boils down to is that we there is an increasing

amount of work which we suggest we would outsource. The other thing to think about is that there are joint ventures and off-set deals as well. With mostly all of the sales campaigns nowadays the airlines, the buyers of these aircrafts, civil particularly, even military, will say, 'yes, we'll buy your engines however we'd like part of the work share.' Or, 'here is some development money up front, we'll give you £x million development money in return for work share on that engine'.

Along with reductions in defence expenditure in the UK and the inevitable cuts in staffing levels that accompany organisational restructuring and the adoption of 'rationalised' production systems, this pattern of outsourcing was a major factor affecting job losses at the JetCo case study plant. In 1980, the plant employed 13,000 workers. By 1990 this had reduced to just over 8000, and by 2001 to 4300. Not long after our fieldwork was completed further losses were announced in a process of gradual 'salami-slicing'. During a later interview in 2006, the plant's AMICUS-AEEU convenor noted that

> The company's 'make-buy' policy was to fall in line with the other major aero-engine company, which was GE. To strategically have a policy of what they were going to make and what they were going to buy from contractors. As a result of that, this plant has suffered badly – along with quite a few other sites that have suffered as well.

Our interviews with JetCo's manual workers, augmented by comments on questionnaires, provided a picture that was remarkably similar to the experiences of their Airframes counterparts. In the context of organisational change and an increasingly assertive management, many workers took umbrage at what they saw as bullying management methods of raising productivity on the shop floor. They also voiced a sense of job insecurity and frustration over lack of consultation. Some examples:

> I really believe that my local management are more interested in output and disciplining their blokes than employee welfare. They don't coach, they push.
>
> (Machinist)

JetCo management has sunk to an all-time low in bullying, dictating and lack of man-management skills. So much so that ninety per cent of my colleagues believe that this plant will be finished as a production unit in ten years. All aspects of working life here, for example, continuous improvement teams and training, have all been used by my managers in an unacceptable way and in a bullying and inept fashion.

(Engine Fitter)

The overall management attitude has changed little over the years. Despite the removal of the old evidence of 'us and them' (separate toilets, canteen, etc.) it still exists and is encouraged by middle management who seem to gain some satisfaction from an air of superiority.

(Tinsmith)

The main problem with JetCo is the lack of job security and the unwillingness of management to tell us what our future holds. Large-scale redundancies have hit morale very hard and there is a large divide between management and the shop-floor.

(Sheetmetal worker)

Non-manual workers articulated similar concerns about management's attempts to drive labour harder, with its inevitable impact on health. They also criticised a lack of consultation which left them with the constant feeling of being 'kept in the dark' about matters that affected their future livelihoods:

There are ever-increasing demands on staff to do more, responsibilities being moved downwards on to supervisory staff from managers or the increasing amount of stress being generally felt by the workforce. The company's drive towards greater productivity from a smaller workforce, and thus greater profit, means that morale is being lowered, stress is being increased and bean counters and consultants are being listened to more than employees.

(Draughtsman)

They're going on about getting a 40-day engine [lead time target]. Now what's the commitment from the shop floor and the staff on this? We don't know what the total commitment's going to be. What will be expected of us? What controls will be put in place over us? So if we're sick, if we're ill, or on our holidays, our family life outside will it be destroyed, will our marriages be destroyed because we've got to work around the clock? All those issues to me are not clear, it's not been explained and it's a worry. For the younger people who've just got married, with young families coming in, it may be yes, they can earn the money, but it could destroy family life.

(Manufacturing Engineer)

So at the moment we're wondering what's the plan? What's going to happen in the future? So when it comes to the broader issues like what the hell's going to happen to the site, why have they brought this chap in, why have they pushed the knowledgeable people out, what are they going to do, why haven't we been consulted, why don't we know about this, what is the plan?

(Test Engineer)

Our questionnaire data reflected these patterns of grievance and discontent. For example, just as we saw at Airframes, the data highlighted a pattern of labour intensification. Four-fifths of both manual and non-manual workers indicated that the degree of flexibility required in their work had increased while nearly 60 per cent of manual workers and three-quarters of non-manual workers indicated an increase in the amount of work they were expected to complete each week. Job insecurity was also relatively high: 44 per cent of non-manual workers and nearly three-quarters of manual workers either disagreed or strongly disagreed with the proposition that their job was secure. And again, as we saw at Airframes, large numbers of workers on the shop floor and in the engineering offices indicated a lack of trust and consultation at work. For example, two thirds of non-manual workers and nearly 90 per cent of manual workers felt that their management believed they were in a separate team to their employees. Equally, over half of non-manual workers and 70 per cent of manual workers felt that they were hardly ever or never consulted on future company plans while nearly three quarters of non-manual workers and nearly 90 per cent of manual workers indicated the same lack of consultation over the question of staffing issues and redundancies.

To sum up, during the five years leading up to our research, workers at both firms became subject to a material change in labour process conditions rooted in a more efficient consumption of their labour power. Design and production functions underwent considerable reorganisation, a process aimed at cutting labour costs and intensifying labour though raising flexibility and task enlargement. These changes did not take hold in an industrial relations vacuum, however. Contemporaneously, management in both firms had sought to legitimise change by exploiting the new industrial relations environment catalysed by New Labour's modernisation project (Martínez Lucio and Stuart, 2002; Stuart and Martínez Lucio, 2005). That is, they attempted to suppress potential trade union opposition by a process of incorporation – developing more co-operative, 'partnership-based' relationships with the principal trade union bargaining groups. It is to this process that we now turn.

Informal workplace partnership: The case of Airframes

The micro-institutional context in which partnership relations were played out at Airframes comprised a mix of conventional bargaining forums operating alongside a more elaborate consultative meeting structure. The plant's two main bargaining groups (covering the manual and non-manual workforce) met management separately on negotiating committees to discuss pay and conditions. The consultative processes took place in a variety of joint management-union forums. These included a multi-site works council, a single site-based company council, and various specialist committees to discuss such questions as workload, future projects, staffing levels, grading schemes, bonus schemes and the use of subcontract and temporary labour.

Patterns of partnership in the UK can be divided essentially into two main forms: the formal and the informal agreement (Bacon and Samuel, 2007; Oxenbridge and Brown, 2002). In the case of Airframes, senior management showed no interest in signing formal agreements. Instead, they emphasised informality with a specific interest in treating partnership as a process, a qualitative change in the nature of management–union relations, rather than a relationship that can be formalised and regulated. The overall aim was to forge a new understanding with trade unions that, in return for greater involvement in managerial discussions governing operational issues, organisational change and strategy, the convenors and senior stewards would accept the need for consensus over questions of plant profitability, cost control and efficiency. In other words, if this was not a return to the business unionism of the 1980s, it was certainly a more unitarist form. Two senior managers commented:

> It is really about being as open and honest with each other as you can. Take the union guys into your confidence and say, 'okay this is the business condition, these are the issues that are facing us. We want to work with you on this one.' And then listen and not just hear what they come back with but then try and work together to try and develop a joint plan on how you implement some of that.
>
> (Human Resources Director)

> I think the one thing you want as a manager is to know that the people who are working for you are motivated by the same sort of ends and goals and things and if you can somehow get them signed up to that then greater involvement in the decision making process is sort of one half of the battle. If they understand why you're doing what you're doing, difficult in some areas, it would make a huge stride forward.
>
> (Avionics Director)

The union response to this challenge was marked by an element of distrust between the manual and non-manual bargaining groups. Our management interviews elicited the common view that the manual union leadership was far more supportive of management-led change compared to their 'difficult' and 'more distrustful' non-manual counterparts. Reflecting this, in one interview the manual group convenor referred to the tensions caused by partnership, 'that my union is very positive on it, whereas MSF have a bigger problem with it but their culture's so different, what they see as important and what we see as important'. In the event, the Airframes manual group leadership arrived at a position of explicit support of the partnership agenda whereas the non-manual group, led by AMICUS-MSF rejected it. The latter argued that management was unlikely to sanction a weakening of its prerogatives or allow independent union agendas to influence company decision-making processes. In this chapter we focus on the response of the pro-partnership manual union group (for a fuller account of these inter-union tensions and different strategic responses, see Danford et al., 2007; 2005).

A number of writers have noted recently the importance of assertive rank and file union leadership styles for shaping more independent and participative union forms (for example, Darlington, 1994; Fairbrother, 1996; Greene et al., 2000); or equally, the implications of its absence (Carter and Poynter, 1999). Much less attention, however, has been directed to the leadership style required for the realisation of managerial conceptualisations of partnership. The pro-partnership group at Airframes provides one such case. It was led by a T&GWU convenor, a charismatic local figure who was active in New Labour politics as well as the union, who took on the role of partnership 'champion'. This was in the face of a good degree of scepticism and antipathy from rank and file members (and some managers too). During a number of interviews he explained how his support for the idea of cooperation with management agendas was based on a principled rejection of traditional collective union power (through strikes) and that its substitution by new forms of union influence at work was more likely to generate gains in the quality of working life of his grassroots members. These interviews were replete with terms and ideas that are not associated with conventional rank and file discourse. For example, 'I don't want power, I want influence', 'we need to raise our competitive game', 'we have to reduce costs', 'we have to compete in the market place' and 'we're trying to move the company forward'. The company's HR Director provided an instructive example of the effect of this new approach:

My personal view is that the relationships are pretty good and have certainly improved and that's taken a lot of time and effort on behalf of both parties in that respect. I think that the [manual] unions have changed in their own approach to life. I think the company, by and large, has also changed its perception that you know the unions aren't just there to cause trouble. We can work together. So I think that, by and large, the relationships are good. Earlier this year we had our production staff convenor standing up and doing a joint presentation with one of the heads of operations to all of the production staff around the company, saying, 'look guys, things aren't that good, looking forward, so we've got to be more flexible, we've got to be prepared to move around etc, etc.' That to me was a fairly significant step forward, from a union environment where that wouldn't have happened a good few years ago.

What impact did partnership have on rank and file interests? In fact, very little that any objective assessment could construe as beneficial. For example, despite management overtures to the effect that partnership would enhance job security by both reducing the threat of job loss and providing unions advance warning of any threat to staffing levels, the company announced 600 redundancies at the plant early in 2002. The scale of job loss came as a complete surprise to both union activists and members. No advance warning or preparatory discussions were in evidence. Three years later in 2005, management declared another 640 job losses. The development of the new, 'qualitatively different' partnership relationship had no impact on the numbers involved or the redundancy process itself.

Another example was the extent of union involvement in decisions governing company restructuring. As we described briefly above, Airframes merged with a major Italian aerospace manufacturer in 2004. Detailed discussions and agreements, in principle governing the nature of the merger and the likely new company structure were completed during the fieldwork phase of our research (during 2001 and 2002). The timing of this 'critical event', with its implications for jobs, individual responsibilities and workloads, enabled us to assess the effectiveness of partnership in providing union (and employee) influence through direct and indirect consultation forums and collective bargaining processes. In fact, our interviews with shop stewards and workers highlighted a widespread feeling that 'employee voice' on this issue was minimal, and for some, non-existent. One worker felt that

> we don't influence that sort of thing. No not really. Things were issued at the time but it did seem to go on a long time and people did seem to feel, 'what is happening, no one's asking us?'. Since it's happened at the beginning of this year, I don't say we've had very much information on it. Even things like what do our Italian colleagues earn, what holidays do they get? I'd like to know that. Well I know they get more bank holidays, Roman Catholic country, I suppose. Well really we couldn't have a big input into it, anyway. At the end of the day it's a corporate issue.

According to another worker:

> I think that type of thing is one of the subjects that's leading to a bit
> of unease and concern for job security in the future and probably the
> worry is that we're not being told anything because the management
> don't have a plan. They're just winging it like everybody else.

The UK's adoption of the EU Works Council Directive required the
newly merged firms to establish an Anglo-Italian council. However,
management at the UK plant resisted this; the preferred company
policy was 'one board and two separate union organisations' as one
MSF steward described it. This was hardly the new spirit of cooperation
that the advocates of partnership might expect. Indeed, such management attitudes – and the lack of effective consultation – affected
the confidence of the manual group leader who gradually came to
realise that the lived experience of partnership rarely matched the
'mutuality' rhetoric:

> Now, we then merged with this Italian company. Now that, to be
> fair, we were in favour of because we believed what we were told.
> Since then I'm now having a few misgivings about it, they build
> aircraft and they're identical to ours ... We haven't had any con-
> tact with Italy, we're not being encouraged to contact them. We've
> been told that we can set up this sort of joint European council
> but nothing has happened about that. The company in my opin-
> ion are keeping us in the dark slightly on that.

Perhaps the most damaging outcome at Airframes was the effect of
partnership on relationships between senior stewards and rank and
file members. Many manual workers we interviewed had no objection
in principle to the concept of 'partnership' in the sense that in an ideal
world, material outcomes of a bargaining relationship between equal
partners are likely to be preferable to strikes, loss of wages and immediate hardship. However, when probed on the experiential dimensions
of management–union relations, the widely articulated view was that
union power and the protection of labour standards had severely
diminished. Moreover, the combination of hollow union participation
and the imposition of managerial prerogatives prompted concerns
about partnership's potential to recast management–union interactions

and weaken the bonds of accountability and trust between steward and member that have long characterized the social relations of workplace unionism on the shop floor (Beynon, 1984; Hyman, 1975). The following comments reflect this:

> It's starting to come to a stage now where people are saying, "well the union are saying yes all the time and getting nothing for it.
> (T&GWU Shop Steward)

> I don't think they're very influential at all, in that regard. I think we've lost all our teeth. I think they get involved quite a bit but how much notice the company actually takes of it I don't know.
> (Inspector)

> Well, all you've got to look at is, who's our union leader? Bloke called Gary Connors ... He's got his little cronies that sit at his little table ... I think that when they go to some of their top echelon meetings with the upper crust, they tend to drop their hats and push their noses up there. That's the impression I've always got.
> (Aircraft Fitter)

> I think it should be more 'them and us' but it seems to be more 'them and them'. Years ago, there used to be more say, you know it would be, 'right we're not happy, so we'll block the road' or whatever. But now it's not like that because somebody else can come along and take your job now. So that's the bottom line I guess.
> (Teamleader)

To sum up, the development of partnership at Airframes was one characterised by informal agreement between management and senior stewards representing manual trade unions. Our analysis uncovered little evidence of 'mutuality' or any semblance of balance of power between the two main partners. Instead, despite the benign discourse governing trade union relationships, management treated partnership in an instrumental fashion, as a means of legitimating change and securing union approval for employer-dominated agendas. As such, it was no surprise that many rank and file members – and local shop stewards – saw no advantages to their new industrial relations environment and, indeed, came to regard partnership with some antipathy. Was such an outcome a function of partnership's immanent contradictions? Or was it instead related to management's preference for informality and 'process'? We consider this question further by turning to the case of JetCo where a formal partnership agreement was in place.

Formal workplace partnership: The case of JetCo

The various forums in which management–union interactions took place on a formal basis were, if anything, more extensive than was the case at Airframes. The plant's two bargaining groups, manual and non-manual, operated separately for the purpose of negotiating pay and conditions. Strategic issues, such as investment strategy, finance, orders, staffing plans and specific business initiatives were covered in different joint consultation forums. In most cases, leading representatives of the manual and non-manual groups sat together in a system of multi-tiered consultation comprising a bi-weekly meeting with HR managers, a monthly meeting with the corporate director of operations, a quarterly meeting of senior management and union representatives in the largest business units, and a twice yearly meeting of a global council. The latter was established in 2005 as a replacement for an earlier hybrid European Works Council. The composition of the global council comprised senior managers and employee representatives from plants in the UK, Europe, North America, South America and Asia. Its purpose was to enable consultation and information-sharing on a range of transnational strategic and policy-based issues. In addition, following the UK government's adoption of the Information and Consultation of Employees Regulations in 2005, the company established a new UK Information and Consultation Council. Reflecting core partnership principles, the remit of the council was to provide early consultation on business issues affecting employees and to provide information and consultation with employees in a way that enabled opinions to be considered before decisions were reached. Matters subject to consultation included future business activities and strategy, the introduction of new working methods, transfers of production, outsourcing and site closures or other job cuts.

The two union groups' strategic orientation towards partnership was the mirror image of the Airframes case. The manual unions rejected partnership on ideological grounds, believing that any union that embraced cooperation with employers betrayed class interests and risked alienating rank and file members. By contrast, the non-manual unions (dominated by AMICUS-MSF) supported partnership in principle (for detailed analysis of the manual unions' more aggressive oppositional stance, see Danford et al., 2007; 2005).

JetCo management's interest in partnership was very similar to the situation at Airframes in that a recasting of union relations was seen as an essential precursor to securing a degree of worker compliance with, or even acceptance of the continuous process of organisational restructuring and rationalisation described above. Indeed, many senior managers we interviewed stressed how partnership should be seen as a psychological process, a battle of 'hearts and minds' that culminates in a permanent realignment of trade union priorities towards core company objectives. We interviewed 15 senior managers and line managers at JetCo and although there were certain nuances in their various interpretations of the partnership concept, the level of agreement on the underlying business case for partnership was striking. That is, partnership was not to be regarded as a contemporary form of establishing worker rights and workplace democracy. Instead, it was a process of changing union behaviour and educating activists about the relationship between market principles and individual responsibilities at work. For example,

> [Partnership] means sitting down together and listening to one another, taking on board alternative proposals, thinking about them, jointly arriving at a way forward that makes sense and that meets as far as is possible all the relevant aspects. That is, a) that the performance of the business does actually improve, b) we do become more effective, c) we do achieve an improvement in customer satisfaction which is we've improved the lead time, we're more responsible, we've enhanced the quality or whatever it is, and d) we've also taken on board the employment aspects, the people aspects.
>
> (HR Director)

An operations director commented:

> I echo the words you said when you first came here about 'what does partnership really mean?', and it's become probably very

difficult because so many people have got different views of what partnership is and we've sort of turned it into how do we work together better ... But there's a number of things in here that talk about how do we begin discussions with trade unions, what are the cost and benefits of a partnership proposal: training and communication behaviours ... also looking at the way the trade union is organised as well. We are six to eight months behind making the progress that we wanted to, we've had several meetings with the trade unions on their framework, and of course it's very difficult because they don't believe that we as management should be telling trade unions how to operate – they don't tell us how to operate, so you know. But there's slow progress being made, and I think the thing about partnership is you've got to involve people in it. You've got to get people involved in the business.

Thus, for JetCo's managers, the underlying logic of partnership was very similar to the Airframes case. That is, the development of cooperative relationships with unions was seen as a stage towards the realignment of union and employee attitudes towards acceptance of practices that raised business efficiency, plant competitiveness and profitability. Unlike Airframes, however, JetCo's managers attempted to make partnership more systematic by establishing a partnership agreement that spelt out concrete mechanisms of joint cooperation. The agreement was signed in 1998 and implemented the following year, after a series of joint workshops convened by an independent partnership 'consultant'. We were given access to the agreement and workshop documentation, analysis of which provides some instructive insights into the nature of typical partnership objectives. For example, it was notable how the written proposals tabled by management were essentially an assertive list of demands for better performance – and labour rationalisation – dressed up in the language of openness and inclusion:

- 'To have the contribution, support and commitment of staff and management to take people through the difficult steps of the necessary change required to achieve a 30 per cent reduction in Engineering time.'
- 'For unions to play a positive and pro-active role to help deliver a common aim.'

- 'MSF and management working together to break down barriers to enable the workforce to be empowered and effective.'
- 'To provide a vehicle for joint discussion and agreement to deliver the required business performance to ensure the future survival of the company and its workforce.'
- 'To adapt our working practices to facilitate business goals. For example, demarcation, flexible working, sub-contractor usage, etc.'

By contrast, although the union side still had considerable organisational strength in terms of membership, density and a long history of organisational independence, the active process of partnership, anchored as it is in the seductive unitarist ideology of 'teamwork' and 'synergy', seemed to have reshaped union concerns into a series of concessionary statements. For example,

- 'To gain trust with management.'
- 'To be involved in important company decisions.'
- 'For management to feel we are not trying to hinder their proposals.'
- 'A collaborative partnership between MSF and Management to save 30 per cent of costs by 2001. The partnership will be based on trust, openness, positive thinking and a genuine desire to find the best possible deal for members and management.'
- 'Job security and increased reward through improved productivity.'
- 'The union shall become the central focus of communication and influence with the company for all of its employees.'

These joint proposals were drafted into a 'collaborative partnership agreement between AMICUS-MSF and JetCo Engineering Management' incorporating mutually agreed statements that seemed to pay little attention to the traditions of union independence, or for that matter, the principle of upholding separate and legitimate interests:

- 'Secure employment and good conditions can be provided only by a successful business. The partnership will endeavour to tackle the challenges of 1999 and beyond in such a way that everyone associated with the business can benefit.'
- 'The partnership will be based upon trust, openness, positive thinking and a genuine desire to work together to achieve our mutual success.'

- 'We feel that the partnership is a significant step forward in our working relationship. We will seek to share our experience and involve other groups and unions as we proceed.'
- 'In this context our first task is to work together to achieve a 30 per cent reduction in Engineering time by December 2000 with a commitment to using all means to avoid compulsory redundancies.'

The agreed machinery of this partnership was the creation of a five-year programme of joint working parties (involving senior managers, AMICUS-MSF representatives and members) to address mutually agreed issues such as reductions in engineering labour time, pay and reward, use of subcontract labour, effective teamworking and employee morale.

What was the impact of this more formal and methodical form of partnership? For the plant's AMICUS-MSF convenor, more constructive engagement in the working parties and the company's broader structure of consultation committees was viewed pragmatically, as a means of regaining at least a measure of the union influence lost during the Thatcher era. Participation was also perceived as an opportunity for recasting the conventional role of the union, from one based on collective constraint against managerial prerogative to something closer to management interests, as a constructive and influential agent:

> The relationship [with management] generally is quite good I think but it has changed quite a lot since the mid-eighties, the Thatcher years, when it was very frosty. Their attitude during those years was whilst they didn't derecognise us, they just ignored us. They didn't communicate with us, always communicated with us last. It would go on for certainly weeks, if not months, without them talking to us at all ...
>
> [With partnership] I think our role changes because we've become an agent of change as opposed to an opposer of change, if it works properly, we become part of the process of changing things, and I think our role within that is to make sure that change doesn't damage our members, that it will in fact benefit our members ... What partners should be able to say is what do we actually need to do, what is the problem, what is the joint solution to the problem, how do we effect the change?

In fact, our research found that these aspirations did not come to fruition. The reasons for this can be linked to the fragility of partnership in the context of deeper tensions in the capitalist employment relationship. Two examples provided here are rooted essentially in questions of employment security and trust.

Maintaining members' jobs and livelihoods lies at the core of trade union interests at work and it is no surprise, therefore, that the question of improving job security became a central concern of the many advocates of workplace partnership in the UK (for example, TUC, 2001 and 1999; IPA, 1997). The partnership agreement at JetCo did not provide any firm guarantees about staffing levels but like many such agreements in the UK (see, for example, Kelly, 2004; Oxenbridge and Brown, 2002) it did provide employment security assurances governing the avoidance of compulsory redundancies and a commitment to advance warning and consultation over potential job losses. In fact, these principles were tested – and were found to be wanting – two years after the completion of the agreement. The JetCo site had been subject to a long-term process of labour shedding. During the 1990s, for example, the workforce had halved from 8000 to 4300 through combinations of mass redundancies and 'salami-slicing' methods. This process was marked by union exclusion from decision-making processes with no advance warning provided or discussion of alternative solutions. The site unions soon discovered that little would change under partnership, however. In 2002, and in the immediate aftermath of the al-Qaeda attacks on New York, management imposed further cuts involving another 1300 job losses overall. During later discussions with AMICUS-MSF and AEEU convenors, we were told how the company had taken advantage of the post-September 11 downturn in aerospace markets by implementing draconian job cuts and ignoring union arguments for alternative solutions.

In the light of this experience of the contradiction between company rhetoric and hard, market-based realities, some union members we interviewed adopted a cynical position on partnership's ability to generate a better employment record:

> Isn't it a fact that, however we package this [partnership], we know that *JetCo*'s shareholders want profits? Company profits and people – that must be the most difficult thing in the world to balance, and I don't think anybody gets that right, do they? That's as far as I can see it. I cannot see the two really coming together

or being made to come together, because on the one hand you need to make a lot of money – that means you need to have fewer people doing more. Fewer – more, fewer – more, for jobs to disappear up 'you know where', but ... it is because 'win-win' means more profits, more shares, meaning a decreasing amount of employees.

(Production Engineer)

I mean, it goes back to people's job security. If they had job security people would say yes, we'll be members of the partnership. But no-one's signing a job security agreement to say that you've got a job for life anymore, people thought they had, but they won't do that anymore.

(Site Engineer)

The second issue concerned the level of trust between managers and workers, a commodity that some regard as the distinctive feature of workplace partnership (Guest and Peccei, 2001). Many of the workers we interviewed spoke about their support for partnership as an idea or aspiration but equally, the predominant view was that high trust was a mirage or mere rhetoric, never matching workers' individual experiences of managerial action. For example,

I think that the company needs to, presumably, convince its workforce that it is on their side, if you like, that they're not just another resource. You come to terms like human resources, which again just creates wrong perceptions. That people are not just a resource along with the machines and the capital employed in the company – that people do count. And that people are valuable. Now we see often the words said, I think one of the things I've noticed over the last, say, five years, is that from the very top level the words are being said – the right words – about the value, how actually employees are valued and the way that the company wants to go as a company. And then you suddenly see that that doesn't seem to cascade down through the management structures and levels. It seems to be that the work carries on as before at the lower levels.

(Production Business Analyst)

The operation of the partnership working parties provided one example of this. Despite the initial support of union representatives and participating members, many of these forums soon lost their initial

momentum and eventually atrophied. One reason for this was a corollary of the organisational restructuring, requiring the plant's operations
and line managers to become directly accountable for unit profitability
and performance on a daily basis. In these circumstances line and middle management demanded a strengthening of its prerogatives and
the flexibility to react unilaterally to market-driven problems and
challenges. For many managers, partnership was both a hindrance
and an irrelevance since they had neither the time nor the inclination
to negotiate or compromise with shop stewards in the interests of joint
cooperation. As one AMICUS-MSF representative put it, 'they have a lot
of different influences which change month by month ... and basically I think it is they who have a problem with partnership because
they cannot necessarily deliver on what they have promised to do'.
But there was a further problem, one that reflects the essence of low
trust management culture in many British workplaces. Many workers
we spoke to in both plants, and in non-manual and manual areas
alike, described an inability on the part of management to relinquish
their sense superiority or class status, something the integrative doc-
trine of partnership could not mask. For example, one JetCo engineer, an AMICUS-MSF nominee on the partnership working parties,
described how he had encountered resistance to the idea that 'run-
of-the-mill' employees could input into decision-making processes
that were held to be the property of management:

> [Management] didn't really want you to go there. I was thinking
> back to these partnerships and one of the impressions I remembered
> was that the management people there struck me as being sort of
> prejudiced and bigoted, and as management people, slightly arro-
> gant and superior. It was like they were the managers, they manage
> these people, so they were obviously superior and intelligent. They
> wanted to preserve that distinction in a way.

Management's use of the consultation committee structure provided
a further example of lack of transparency and trust. In 2005, the company introduced a national Information and Consultation Council
in response to the EC Directive on Information and Consultation in
the Workplace. The new council's remit was to provide early consultation on business issues affecting employees and to provide information
and consultation with employees in a way that enabled opinions to

be considered before decisions were reached. Issues subject to consultation included future business activities and strategy, the introduction of new working methods and job cuts. Leaders of both main bargaining groups took the decision to place less experienced shop stewards on this committee, partly to give them experience but also because the new council was perceived as yet another layer of consultation which exacerbated the already excessive demands on their time caused by participation on the company's many existing forums. During our later visits to the plant in 2006, the senior stewards described how they came to regret this decision. Rather than act in a spirit of openness and trust, management attempted to exploit the new forum by engineering a shift in the nature and locale of collective bargaining. Specifically, negotiations governing a number of contractual issues that traditionally fell within the remit of plant-level collective bargaining were moved to the new national council and implemented once 'consultation' had taken place. These included the use of agency labour, changes to a redundancy agreement, the standardisation of UK conditions, the payment of holiday pay to retirees and job transfers. JetCo's AEEU-MSF convenor commented:

> We've got an agreement dating back to 2000 on redundancy terms, which contains some elements the company say will fall foul of the ageism regulations. We are not absolutely sure, but that's what they say. They used the UK Council to discuss that, even though they were told by the people on it that it was a bargaining issue. They nevertheless consulted them and then decided, having consulted them, these were now the new terms they were going to put in place ... In our view, the company has abused the UK Council by talking to them about something which should have been bargained.

In the case of the redundancy agreement, in response to union protestations the company was forced to retreat and place the issue back on the plant bargaining agenda. Nevertheless, seven years after the signing of the formal partnership agreement, what emerged was an attempt to exploit inexperienced shop stewards by substituting national consultation for plant bargaining. This was seen as yet another breach in the much heralded trust relationship that workplace partnership is supposed to engender.

To sum up, although JetCo's formal agreement contained the potential to establish more cohesive and durable partnership relationships compared to the Airframes case, material outcomes for the signatory union and its members seemed little better. Over time, trade union influence through participation in the partnership working parties and consultation forums waned. At best, these different partnership forums came to be seen as mere talking shops. And at worse, in the context of extant low trust relations, they were exploited by different sets of managers who, rather than embrace the notion of power-sharing, were more intent on strengthening their own prerogatives and placing strict limits on union influence.

Conclusion

In this chapter we have analysed the introduction of two different forms of workplace partnership (formal and informal) in the context of contemporary corporate restructuring in the UK aerospace industry, the nature of which produced a radical effect on organisational form and labour deployment. There were two core dimensions to this restructuring. The first was the rapid development of transnational joint ventures, strategic alliances and sometimes full mergers between different capitals. The second was the rationalisation of production and jobs by a combination of stripping out labour from design and manufacturing processes, downsizing plants into a plethora of financially accountable profit centres and introducing a range of 'high performance' labour flexibility measures. For labour, the upshot of these changes was a widespread exposure to job shedding at both case study plants and for 'survivors', a deterioration in the quality of working life manifest in patterns of work intensification, stress and multiple concerns over job content and tenure. Our survey and interview data found that many workers experienced increases in the volume of work they were expected to complete each week, increases in task flexibility, growing job insecurity and frustration over the lack of consultation on a range of issues that affected their careers and livelihoods.

The many managers we interviewed at both plants made no attempt to obscure the realities of these changes or to deny their implications for the regulation of the employment relationship. The dominant view was that in the context of intense competitive pressures in the sector and the increasing challenges posed by airline customers and defence procurement processes alike, management required sufficient room for manoeuvre to respond rapidly to market exigencies. As with many cases elsewhere in British industry, the development of partnership at the case study plants should, therefore, be viewed against this backdrop of market turbulence and organisational restructuring (Kelly, 2004). Senior managers were not hostile to trade unions in an absolute sense (unlike many greenfield employers, for instance). They seemed sincere in their interest in partnership and were prepared to offer greater union input into strategic management processes. But only on the employer's terms, something that we have described as 'the business case for partnership' (Danford et al., 2005, pp. 138–44). Union participation was viewed, principally, as a means of securing some semblance of shop steward support of business objectives rather than offering the prospect of greater union influence rooted in more independent organising agendas. To put this another way, the two sets of management were happy to offer unions a degree of institutional centrality at the workplace (Terry, 2003) but only if the consequent form of union activity offered no challenge to managerial authority.

Unlike many appraisals of partnership which tend to both understate the interests of rank and file members and exclude their experiences from research designs (see, for example, Samuel, 2007), our analysis of the direct accounts of workers themselves found that the partnership 'balance-sheet' was decidedly negative. Whether established as an informal arrangement, as was the case with Airframes, or as a formal partnership agreement, as was the case with JetCo, the partnership process did nothing to stem the pattern of job losses at both plants, or to offer early warning mechanisms in advance of rationalisation decisions, or to offer the prospect of discussions on alternative solutions. Equally, despite the powerful 'mutual gains' rhetoric which is clearly embedded in notions of high trust in the employment relationship, partnership did nothing to diminish management's sense of class status and primacy over subordinates, what many workers still referred to as 'us and them'. As a result, union and worker influence within the consultative forums established by the formal partnership at JetCo eventually weakened considerably. At Airframes, the construction of closer ties between the workplace union leadership and management under the informal partnership arrangement catalysed a new problem of trust – the distancing of the rank and file from union leaders.

From the viewpoint of grassroots members then, partnership came to be seen not just as an irrelevant localised union strategy for countering corporate power, but also as an instrument for further weakening the collective defence of labour standards and conditions at work.

7
Whither Partnership?

We have suggested in this book that partnership is rooted in government and employer strategies to redefine industrial relations. This is as a precursor to closing the UK productivity gap and 'modernising' public services. Partnership is the chosen vehicle for a renewed capital accumulation strategy predicated on 'progressive workplace consensus' as an alternative to the traditional adversarial industrial relations regime. The TUC, by offering a productivity coalition to employers in the interest of organisational and national competitiveness, promotes partnership as a route back to union renewal and societal legitimacy. Such strategic reorientation implies a shift in belief systems about the employment relationship and the world of work. This third way or 'new pluralist' ideology deregisters class conflict and is justified by an appeal to risk minimisation in a globalising economy. For unions the negation of separate interests in favour of mutual interests is a risky proposition but is confronted by the TUC in an acknowledgement of difference between 'good' and 'bad' partnership, whereby only the six principles of 'good' partnership (itself predicated on 'strong' unions) are supported. Our case studies were designed to test the reality of partnership in both unionised and non-unionised environments and to assess the sustainability of the partnership model in practice. In particular, we were keen to register the everyday experience of employees. To undertake our research objectives we utilised surveys and interviews and explored key aspects of the partnership paradigm such as task discretion, job satisfaction and perceived job security. We also attempted to contextualise the studies by recording the industrial relations regimes in each organisation, and noting the changes as partnership was applied. Of course, there are limitations to this research technique, as we can only record the reality of partnership as it exists, but cannot determine 'what might have been' without partnership.

In Chapter 2 we provide detailed statistical evidence of our conclusions. We find some evidence of positive worker outcomes. These were mainly in those establishments which had already adopted a good quota of high-performance work practices in recent years, such as sections of the aerospace industry. Skills and responsibilities have increased in all sectors, as has task discretion. As a result, the general feeling of job satisfaction was high when measured by themes of job influence, sense of achievement and supervisory relations. Some caveats need to be expressed. Task discretion was much higher over how tasks would be completed as opposed to what tasks should be done. In other words the empowerment can only be expressed as *power to do* tasks but not *power over* tasks (see Nelson and Wright, 1994). Similarly, discretion was more apparent in higher grades than lower, and for skilled grades rather than semi-skilled or unskilled. Similar variations according to grade and status were found for job satisfaction, with those at the higher end more likely to express satisfaction than those lower down the hierarchy. A polarisation was thus observed between higher skill and lower skill jobs in terms of both task discretion and job satisfaction. We also found sectoral differences in job satisfaction, with the finance sector performing better than aerospace and the public sector. Our generally positive scores for job satisfaction are tempered, however, by negative employee outcomes in the realm of work intensification and stress. We present clear evidence that workers are feeling more stressed and are working harder through both intensification and extensification of work. This is apparent in all sectors, and across all grades, but with greater reports of stress in the public sector organisations. Although we did not measure worker productivity directly, it is clear that work intensification would have acted to increase individual worker output, and thus fulfil government and employer objectives. We have observed distinct feelings of increased job insecurity, which have been substantiated by actual job loss in some organisations. Our private sector case organisations had all suffered at the hand of incessant corporate restructuring and/or instability in governance through takeovers, mergers and alliances. The ensuing restructuring inevitably led to job loss as shareholder interests were maximised. In local government we found that job loss was worse in areas where partnership had been introduced as part of 'Best Value' in comparison to those areas where it had not. With these conclusions any notion of partnership as a process of risk sharing between employer and employee appears incredulous, as the risks are taken solely by employees.

Consensus, consultation and ideology

We have highlighted the centrality of consensus and consultation in partnership practice. For advocates of partnership, consensus and consultation should lead to more employee involvement in organisation affairs and more control over work itself. This is the essence of mutual gain, which should not only have a material base in shared benefits of job security and income but also in softer variables associated with quality of working life. We find that although the institutions and processes of employee involvement and participation are well embedded in all our organisations, management were mostly regarded by employees as good in providing information, but poor in allowing employees to influence or change decisions. This was especially true for the growing number of agency staff. As Hyman (2005, p. 259) puts it in his critique of Hirschman (1970), 'There is a familiar and chilling phrase: "I hear what you say". The corollary is: "I will take absolutely no notice"'. Moreover, where unions were involved in the process, employee regard for the reality of workplace democracy was weaker in those areas where partnership was practiced than in those areas in which traditional adversarialism lingered. The inability of management to release anything more than information was a product of strict performance regimes imposed from above. Such performance regimes were driven by external pressures, either product market competition in the case of the private sector organisations, or cost and efficiency concerns in the public sector. We suggest that the high-performance model, situated as it is in a neoliberal managerial rhetoric, does not – and cannot – deliver on its ostensible 'win-win' agenda.

We have argued that ideology is central to the process of partnership and its future. More pertinently, a perceived need for change in belief systems is directed by government and employers at employees and their trade unions. We recognise that workplace relations within adversarial processes are a balance of conflict and cooperation between employees and management. For this reason, it is reasonable to assume that both employees and employers are likely to support the 'concept' of partnership as a *modus vivendi*, if for no other reason than it gives an easier and stress free working life and appeals to 'common sense'. But we also recognise that conflict persists, and that the advocates of partnership seek to suppress conflict as a legitimate expression of worker interests. It is in this contradictory space that new ideological frameworks about the world at work can be shaped by those willing to try. From the evidence of government statements and documents it would appear that New Labour have taken to this task, with the promotion of a TW 'progressive workplace consensus'. So how can we determine if the 'consensus' espoused by former Prime Minister Blair as an alternative to conflict has taken root in British industrial relations? Our own results indicate poor effectiveness of employee communication and lead us to conclude that employee involvement is prioritised by management in its negative rather than positive sense. It is used, as Ramsay (1996) has suggested in other cases, to shape employees' attitudes so that employees are more likely to accept change as the imposition of management will. As such the process of partnership is imbued with an ideology that challenges the concrete reality of everyday work. We find limited staff consultation in all our partnership organisations in every sector. Employees mostly indicated that they were hardly ever or never consulted on work practices with very little consultation over staffing issues and pay. There is also polarisation between occupational groups with line managers and, for some themes, non-manual workers, indicating greater consultation than the two manual worker groups. In all our case study organisations there is thus a lack of real and equal dialogue about key aspects of the business. Rather than pointing to social cohesion in the workplace, our study indicates instead a process of worker exclusion. This exclusion flows not only from the realities of workplace democracy, or rather the lack of it, but also from workers' real fears of job insecurity and workplace stress. This exclusion from real power, while apparent in decision-making processes, is even more acute in key distributive issues.

For the trade unions in our case study organisations the key question is whether or not their participation in partnership had led to enhanced union performance within the organisation. We sought to explore whether or not trade unions had strengthened their position within the organisation by engaging with partnership, either through increased power and influence or enhanced member participation and growth. We find that union performance, measured by the service provided to members and communication, was stronger in the aerospace sector than in our public service establishments. We explain this as being the result of a stronger union presence within aerospace, reflecting the historical development of unionism, a more combative tradition and stronger workplace union leadership. Union influence over management, pay and conditions was also higher in the aerospace establishments. Our public sector examples, and the one unionised organisation in finance, have less combative union histories and lower consciousness of workers 'for themselves'. But most importantly, across all the unionised organisations, we find that working in a partnership environment is negatively associated with union performance. We detect this not only in reduced or constrained ability of the unions to tackle work intensification and job loss, but also in the establishment of emergent divisions between local union leaderships and the rank-and-file members. At Airframes, for example, while many manual workers had no objection to the concept of partnership, the experience of work intensification and redundancies led to a widely articulated view that union power and the protection of labour standards had severely diminished. This led to a weakening of trust between steward and member. In JetCo the partnership agreement pursued by the non-manual workers focussed on job security and resulted in the company providing assurances against compulsory redundancies. The non-manual union side was heavily influenced by the senior steward, who appeared committed to utilising partnership as a 'dented shield' against the vagaries of intensifying international competition by creating a productivity initiative within the company. When the company ignored its own assurances and imposed redundancies after the September 2001 attack on the twin towers the union membership responded with cynicism at the hollowness of partnership as a way forward. At worse, and after a waning of the partnership initiatives, union stewards felt they were exploited by different sets of managers who were intent on strengthening their own prerogatives and placing strict limits on union influence through the partnership process. A similar pattern of initial partnership endorsement was apparent in our local authority case study, where budgetary constraints were feared by the local union leaderships, and partnership through Best Value was encouraged as a defensive union strategy to keep services 'in-house'. The reality is that jobs were not secured by this approach, and the unions appeared to have suffered by their reliance on passivity in the face of the management agendas set within the Best Value framework. A similar story is evident in our NHS trust, where senior stewards had signed up for partnership but remained disappointed with its outcomes. Union activists more critical to the concept of partnership had been marginalised in the process. Stewards also became divorced from their members as partnership progressed, with most ordinary members unaware that they were meant to be in partnership leaving the stewards with constrained ability to contest its outcomes. Within our two finance sector organisations the union at InsuranceCo found that the management strategy was to include the union in a cooperation pact as the means of managing workplace change. This was a largely one-way exchange of moderation on the union's part while the company was unwilling to concede union influence in the traditional bargaining agenda or beyond it. Union members remained committed to union representation although were not uncritical of their union leadership. Workplace representatives were considered insufficiently assertive – as opposed to incorporated – and remote so that members' involvement was passive. The union's resources and orientation towards organising, however, were constrained by the cooperation agreement. Finally, at our non-union example of partnership, FinanceCo, the Partners' Council (PC) was instituted by management with three main objectives: to achieve employee commitment to corporate goals, accommodate legal obligations, and to sustain union avoidance. The PC was not seen as independent or relevant and most employees were not interested in its affairs. The HR department dominated the agenda setting and regarded the PC as an adjunct to other 'two way' means of communicating company priorities to staff. Most importantly, its composition did not inspire employee confidence that grievances could be voiced without retribution. Given these generally negative views of partnership from employees in our organisations, how now can we judge its efficacy?

Partnership and reality transcendence

As we outline in our introductory chapter the TUC case for 'good' partnership is predicated on its six principles and the inclusion of 'strong' trade unions. Interestingly, one of our case study organisations (CityCo) has been referred to by the TUC and its associated Partnership Institute as positive examples of partnership. At CityCo the TUC and the Local Government Employers' Organisation reported on a pilot partnership initiative to demonstrate that 'A key outcome is that the process of partnership has resulted in a new, more constructive union–management relationship based on joint problem-solving' (TUC/EO, 1999). The partnership approach subsequently faltered and failed to develop at corporate level. Our evidence from employees' everyday, lived experience of partnership in practice is extensive and rigorous, and gives insights as to why partnership might potentially wither on the vine as the realities of the partnership arrangements turn to disaffection from the process among the rank and file. We also need to find explanations for shortcomings from the evidence of other case studies. Where 'good' partnership exists with 'strong' union presence, the reality of workplace bargaining may mean that actual industrial relations practices by the unions are little removed from past adversarial traditions. Following Kelly (2005) this may be tested by studying outcomes from the distinction between 'labour parity' and 'employer dominant' partnership whereby we might expect to find more evidence of employee gains in the former as opposed to the latter. However, when he examined matched sectoral pairs of partnership and non-partnership agreements Kelly found that for 'labour parity' types such as that agreed at Borg Warner, the gains for unions, while outstripping the non-partnership match, were as much a product of union power obtained through increased membership and better shop floor organisation than through partnership practice itself. We might suspect that in such cases there might be little difference between what might be labelled 'good' partnership and the 'shrewd' collective bargaining identified by Martínez Lucio and Stuart (2000, p. 21), with partnership expressed merely as a rhetorical adjunct to the bargaining process, rather than an alternative industrial relations framework. Such a distinction would also correspond with the evidence of 'nurturing' partnership identified by Oxenbridge and Brown (2002, p. 273) whereby informal partnership arrangements had been developed on management initiative and where the management strategy was to seek 'greater control over communication structures ... and to shift worker loyalty away from the union, but [where] unions retained an active role on employment regulation'. In a later article, Oxenbridge and Brown (2004b, p. 192) take their analysis further and distinguish between 'robust' partnership arrangements where the union is strong and 'union interviewees ... were more likely to feel that the union had a high degree of influence at the early stage of decision-making processes' and 'shallow' partnerships which 'confer few benefits to one party – the union'. While stewards in the 'robust' cases experienced a greater sense of legitimacy and security in their organisations (Oxenbridge and Brown, ibid., p. 196) they also began to feel isolated from their membership due to confidentiality restrictions while managers appreciated the partnership arrangements as a way to 'soften' the management of change. In such cases, which have clear parallels with our own case study organisations, we would suggest that 'good partnership' acts as a vehicle for workplace restructuring but in the process detaches the local workplace union leadership from its members, running the risk of steward isolation and rank-and-file rejection as the promised material gains of mutuality fail to be delivered.

If 'good' partnership is proving illusory how can this be explained? The simplest explanation may be that the TUC's six principles did not pertain to the case studies under question, but this prospect would seem to be annulled by the TUC's endorsement for some of our case studies (and, indeed, others which may have been critiqued in other research studies). A second explanation may lie in the lack of institutional capacity. This is a view expressed by Terry and Smith (2003) in their argument that in many European countries 'consultation' is viewed by the partners as a more serious business than in the UK, with strong institutional support from the state. However, precisely because of this, it is difficult to disentangle the European institutions of codetermination from that of employee and union bargaining arrangements. There is overlap between the process of 'negotiation' and 'consultation' between unions and employers, and Works Councillors and managements, which makes a comparative measurement of partnership difficult. A more pertinent explanation lies in the nature of political economy and the difficulties of fulfilling the new capital accumulation strategy favoured by New Labour. Indeed, the difficulties of introducing effective high-performance systems, for example, are recognised by practitioners. Porter and Ketels' (2003) government-commissioned report on UK competitiveness suggested that UK companies are less likely to adopt modern management techniques than their competitors. The role of line managers in implementing the process is crucial, and it is here that some resistance to relaxing control may take place. Findings from WERS 2004 would seem to confirm the constraints, as the proportion of workplaces utilising a combination of high-involvement practices has shown only a 'marginal increase' since the 1998 survey (Kersley et al., 2006). Most importantly there appeared a continued lack of trust between employers and employees. 'Trust' is presented as an essential ingredient of high-performance working but it was registered positively in only a 'minority' of workplaces. A 2006 CIPD Survey of 2000 employees confirms the WERS pessimism about the reluctance of British managers to engage seriously with their employees. The survey finds that 30 per cent of employees say they rarely or never get feedback on their performance; only 38 per cent of employees say directors and senior managers treat them with respect and that 42 per cent of employees do not feel they are kept well informed about what's going on in their organisation (CIPD, 2006b).

We are not suggesting that the failure of partnership is due to a pathological reluctance of British managers to engage (although there may be some truth in this). The reasons for reluctant management lie in the continuing structural problems of UK industry. In particular, the corporate turbulence due to continuing shareholder value short-termism makes it particularly difficult to establish job security and trust (Sisson, 1995; Driffield, 1999; Upchurch and Danford, 2001). This point is well recognised by no less than the TUC's ex-General Secretary John Monks (now General Secretary of the ETUC) in his Aneurin Bevan memorial lecture given in November 2006. Monks, the erstwhile foremost advocate of partnership, states:

> Partnership with who? There has been a disintegration of the social nexus between worker and employer – a culture containing broad rights and obligations. The new capitalism wants none of it … I did not fully appreciate what was happening on the other side of the table … it cannot be easy running a firm … when you are up for sale every day and night of the year.
>
> (Monks, 2006)

Further, Monks argued that the short term behaviour of 'overpaid corporate executives' was 'shameless … more and more they resemble Bourbons – and they should be aware of what eventually happened to the Bourbons (Monks, 2006). In reassessing the 'UK Model' ten years on from the original paper published in 1994, Rubery et al. (2005)

seem to confirm that there remains a lack of institutional support for the type of high-performance model so desired by the government. While progress might have been made in educational provision and training in order to boost human capital, Britain has not taken up the necessary aspects of the (increasingly fragile) Rhenish model of institutional support for the high road route to business competitiveness. The long-term decline of manufacturing and its steady replacement with a service economy may also have affected capacity to reach the target model so that 'it may be argued that the opportunities to move onto a high value added manufacturing development path were already lost' (Rubery et al., 2005, p. 31). This does not mean to say, of course, that the search for productivity improvement in UK industry is likely to be fruitless, but rather that it is more likely to continue to come from more intensive and extensive exploitation of the existing workforce than from 'enlightened' policies of employee engagement. As such, adversarialism is alive and well in UK workplaces, enacted by the majority of UK managers if not always by the union side.

Our analysis leads us to suggest that even 'good' partnership in the UK is an illusory concept. In fact, what we identify is a process of reality transcendence whereby the claimed mutuality of partnership breaks down in the face of the imperatives of shareholder interest, profit maximisation and 'cost efficiency' in the public services. Such reality transcendence is central to the TW objectives of risk minimisation through productivity coalitions at the workplace. While productivity may improve, mutuality is sacrificed as work is intensified and job insecurity increases. Such a conundrum between reality and myth is bridged by the ideology of mutuality and harmony of interest that is dependent on the employees' acceptance of the secondary importance of solidaristic and collectivist frames of reference in the workplace. As such it assumes a depoliticisation of workplace relations in the tradition of 'end of ideology' ideology. Such is the essence of TW thinking, which Giddens has called a form of 'utopian realism' in which 'radical democratisation, affecting many spheres of social life, and perhaps extending right up to the global level, can be achieved' (Giddens, 1990).

It can also be argued that the concept of partnership is rooted in liberal 'reasoning of reason' whereby any form of emancipation 'from below' in the Marxist sense is replaced by support for state activity which encourages individual liberty 'from above'. Indeed, Coats (2004), writing from a labour perspective in his piece for the Work Foundation, also expresses this utopianism when he suggests that trade unions should be a source of both bonding and bridging social capital – bonding capital in terms of developing inter-colleague solidarity, and bridging capital in terms of seeking common cause between employee and employer. 'All of this contributes to the "ontological security" that Giddens deems necessary for social cohesion – workers understand their place in the world and have a sufficient sense of continuity to withstand the vicissitudes of their working lives' (Coats, 2004, p. 38). It is this denial of the material basis of the production process, and its consequent social relations and antagonisms that posits partnership as a utopian project. The discourse of partnership has a formalistic negation of content, which places itself outside the process of historical development – even while appearing to emphasise change and dynamism. We can also describe this as separation between a willed end or goal, and means for achieving it. Gramsci (1971) notes that a vital question to ask of a politician's will for a different type of society in the future, a new balance of forces, is

> whether what "ought to be" is arbitrary or necessary; whether it is concrete will on the one hand or idle fancy, yearning, daydream on the other. The active politician is a creator, an initiator; but he neither creates from nothing nor does he move in the turbid void of his own desires and dreams.

Only he who 'bases himself on effective reality' demonstrates concrete will (p. 172). Our case studies are imbued with the difficulties of establishing harmony of interest when the everyday realities of corporate competition and behaviour transpire. Competition between capitals in an increasingly internationalised product market means that individual capitals must continue to exercise their authority over labour in order to increase individual value added and productivity. Of course, an appeal to mutuality and partnership with employers makes common sense, especially when such 'common sense' is supported by government and employer discourse. However, when the realities of partnership unfold it should come as no surprise that workers may resist the temptation to 'understand their place in the world' and reject the partnership paradigm.

Notes

1. Partnership at Work

1. No figures exist for what might be termed 'informal' partnership arrangements.
2. www.ipa-involve.com (accessed 12 December 2006).
3. http://www.eef.org.uk/UK/preview/policy/public/publication21112003. htm (accessed 1st December 2006).
4. www.tuc.org.uk/pi/research.htm (accessed 14 March 2003).
5. Authors' interview with officers of the TUC Partnership Institute (2002).
6. Debates on corporate governance have also crystallised under New Labour within the guise of stakeholderism, theorised in the varieties of capitalism literature and politicised by writers such as Michel Albert and Will Hutton. What is intriguing is the capriciousness of many TW politicians and academics towards the stakeholder vision. The 'individual' version of stakeholderism concentrates on outlining the need to boost education and training so that everyone is provided with the opportunity to participate in the new global economy. As Soskice (1996) argued, this is essentially a New Labour market contract between the government and individuals whereby the state will take on the responsibility of establishing a framework in which learning and mass higher education can take place. As for business, in this scenario, its role is restricted to harnessing the creative skills and competencies of individuals through participation and cooperative working (or partnership). The incoming New Labour government was committed to this watered-down version of stakeholding, heavy on individual learning but stripped of its governance aspects or any critique of power relations within the workplace. As Coates (2000) recorded, by the 1997 General Election even the term 'stakeholding' had been excluded from the Labour Party Manifesto. What was left of the stakeholding discourse were references to 'partnership' as an alternative to conflict between employers and employees, and encouragement of Employee Share Ownership schemes and cooperatives.

4. Best Value in a Local Authority

An earlier version of this chapter was published as 'Best Value and Workplace Partnership in Local Government', *Personnel Review* Vol. 34, No. 6, 2005, pp. 713–28. The contract with Emerald Publishing Group kindly allows its authors to publish elsewhere without having to obtain written permission.

1. The employee surveys included questions taken from the Workplace Employment Relations Survey (WERS98) to allow some comparison with the national data set.
2. In response to recommendations arising from the first and second Best Value inspections, in 2001 and 2002, generic working was gradually dropped in favour of utilising teams of dedicated and specialised staff.

References

Ackers, P. (2002) 'Reframing Employment Relations: The Case for Neo-Pluralism', *Industrial Relations Journal*, 33(1): 2–19.

Ackers, P., Marchington, M., Wilkinson, A. and Dundon, T. (2005) 'Partnership and Voice, with or without Trade Unions: Changing UK Management Approaches to Organizational Participation', in M. Martínez Lucio and M. Stuart (eds) *Partnership and Modernisation in Employment Relations*, Basingstoke: Palgrave Macmillan, pp. 23–45.

Ackers, P. and Payne, J. (1998) 'British Trade Unions and Social Partnership: Rhetoric, Reality and Strategy', *The International Journal of Human Resource Management*, 9(3): 529–50.

Ackers, P. and Wilkinson, A. (2003) 'Introduction: The British Industrial Relations Tradition – Formation, Breakdown and Salvage', in P. Ackers and A. Wilkinson (eds) *Understanding Work and Employment: Industrial Relations in Transition*, Oxford: OUP, pp. 1–32.

Ackroyd, S. and Procter, S. (1998) 'British Manufacturing Organisation and Workplace Industrial Relations: Some Attributes of the New Flexible Firm', *British Journal of Industrial Relations*, 36(2): 163–83.

Allen, T. J. (1986) 'Organizational Structure, Information Technology, and R&D Productivity', *IEEE Transactions on Engineering Management*, 33: 212–17.

Almeida, B. (1997) 'Are Good Jobs Flying Away? U.S. Aircraft Engine Manufacturing and Sustainable Prosperity', *Working Paper No. 206*. The Jerome Levy Economics Institute of Bard College, New York.

Almeida, B. (2001) 'Good Jobs Flying Away from US? The U.S. Jet-Engine Industry', in W. Lazonick and M. O'Sullivan (eds) *Corporate Governance and Sustainable Prosperity*. Basingstoke: Palgrave Macmillan.

Appelbaum, E., Bailey, T., Berg, P. and Kalleberg, A. L. (2000) *Manufacturing Advantage: Why High Performance Work Systems Pay Off*, Ithaca, New York: Cornell University Press.

Archer, R. (1996) 'Towards Economic Democracy in Britain', in P. Hirst and S. Khilnani (eds) *Reinventing Democracy*, Oxford: Blackwell, pp. 85–96.

Ashton, D. and Sung, J. (2002) *Supporting Workplace Learning for High Performance Working*, ILO.

Atkinson, J. (1984) 'Manpower Strategies for Flexible Organization', *Personnel Management*, August: 28–31.

Audit Commission (2002) 'Local Taxation Re-Inspection', May 2002.

Bach, S. (2004) 'Employee Participation and Union Voice in the NHS', *Human Resource Management Journal*, 14(2): 3–19.

Bacon, N. and Samuel, P. (2007) 'Partnership Agreement Adoption, Form and Survival in Britain', *Paper presented to the IIRA 8th European Congress, Manchester*, 3–6 September 2007.

Bain, P. and Taylor, P. (2001) 'Two Steps Forward, One Step Back: Interest Definition, Organisation and Deflected Mobilisation amongst Call Centre Workers'. *Paper presented to the 19th International Labour Process Conference*, Royal Holloway College, London, 26–8 March.

Bain, P. and Taylor, P. (2003) 'Ringing the Changes? Union Recognition and Organisation in Call Centres in the UK Finance Sector', *Industrial Relations Journal*, 33(3): 246–61.

Barley, S. and Kunda, G. (2004) *Gurus, Hired Guns and Warm Bodies: Itinerant Experts in a Knowledge Economy*, Princeton and Oxford: Princeton University Press.

Batt, R. and Appelbaum, E. (1995) 'Worker Participation in Diverse Settings: Does the Form Affect the Outcome, and If So, Who Benefits?', *British Journal of Industrial Relations*, 33(3): 353–78.

Beale, D. (2005) 'The Promotion and Prospects of Partnership at Work at Inland Revenue: Employer and Union Hand-in-Hand', in M. Stuart and M. Martínez Lucio (eds) *Partnership and Modernisation in Employment Relations*, London: Routledge, pp. 137–55.

Beck, U. (1992) *Risk Society: Towards a New Modernity*. Translated by M. Ritter, London: Sage.

Bélanger, J. and Edwards, P. (2007) 'The Conditions Promoting Compromise in the Workplace', *British Journal of Industrial Relations*, 45(4): 713–34.

Bélanger, J., Giles, A. and Murray, G. (2002) 'Towards a New Production Model: Potentialities, Tensions and Contradictions', in Murray, G., Bélanger, J., Giles, A. and Lapointe, P. A. (eds) *Work and Employment Relations in the High-Performance Workplace*, London and New York: Continuum.

Bélanger, J., Lapointe, P. A. and Lévesque, B. (2002) 'Workplace Innovation and the Role of Institutions', in Murray, G., Bélanger, J., Giles, A. and Lapointe, P. A. (eds), Beynon, H. (1984) *Working for Ford*. Second Edition. Harmondsworth: Penguin.

Black, S. and Lynch, L. (2000) 'What's Driving the New Economy: The Benefits of Workplace Innovation', *National Bureau of Economic Research Working Paper 7479*, Revised Version, October.

Black, S. and Lynch, L. (2001) 'How to Compete: The Impact of Workplace Practices and Information Technology on Productivity', *Review of Economics and Statistics*, 83(3): 434–45.

Blair, T. (1998) *Foreword* to *Fairness at Work*, London: DTI, Cmnd 3968, HMSO.

Bluestone, B., Jordan, P. and Sullivan, M. (1981) *Aircraft Industry Dynamics: An Analysis of Competition, Capital and Labor*, Boston, Massachusetts: Aubern House.

Blyton, P. and Turnbull, P. (1998) *The Dynamics of Employee Relations*, Second edition, Basingstoke: Macmillan Business.

Boxall, P. and Purcell, J. (2003) *Strategy and Human Resource Management*, Basingstoke: Palgrave Macmillan.

Braddon, D. (2000) *Exploding the Myth? The Peace Dividend, Regions and Market Adjustment*, Amsterdam: Harwood Academic Publishers.

Brown, P. and Lauder, H. (2001) *Capitalism and Social Progress: The Future of Society in a Global Economy*, Basingstoke: Palgrave Macmillan.

Brown, W. (2000) 'Putting Partnership into Practice in Britain', *British Journal of Industrial Relations*, 38: 299–316.

Bryson, A. (2000) 'Have British Workers Lost Their Voice, or Have They Gained a New One?' *PSI Research Discussion Paper 2*, London: Policy Studies Institute.

Bryson, A. (2001) 'The Foundation of "Partnership"? Union Effects on Employee Trust in Management', *National Institute Economic Review*, 176: 91–104, April 2001.

Bryson, A. (2003) 'Employee Desire for Unionisation in Britain and Its Implications for Union Organising', *PSI Research Discussion Paper 12*, London: Policy Studies Institute.

Bryson, A. (2004) 'Managerial Responsiveness to Union and Non-Union Workers' Voice in Britain', *Industrial Relations*, 43(1): 213–41.

Budd, J. (2004) *Employment with a Human Face*, New York: Cornell University Press.

Burchell, B. (2002) 'The Prevalence and Redistribution of Job Insecurity and Work Intensification', in B. Burchell, D. Ladipo and F. Wilkinson (eds) *Job Insecurity and Work Intensification*, London: Routledge.

Callinicos, A. (2001) *Against the Third Way*, Cambridge: Polity.

Carter, B. and Poynter, G. (1999) 'Unions in a Changing Climate: MSF and Unison Experiences in the New Public Sector', *Industrial Relations Journal*, 30: 499–513.

Catney, P. (2002) 'New Labour and Associative Democracy', *Paper given to the Political Studies Association Conference*, Aberdeen, 5–7 April.

Chandler, J., Berg, E. and Barry, J. (2003) 'Workplace Stress in the United Kingdom: Contextualising Difference', in C. Peterson (ed.) *Work Stress: Studies of the Context, Content and Outcomes of Stress*, New York: Baywood Publishing Company Inc.

Chartered Institute of Personnel and Development (2006a) *Absence Management: A Survey Report*, London: CIPD.

Chartered Institute of Personnel and Development (2006b) 'How Engaged are British Employees?' *Annual Survey Report 2006*, London: CIPD.

Clark, A., Oswald, A. and Warr, P. (1996) 'Is Job Satisfaction U-Shaped in Age?', *Journal of Occupational and Organisational Psychology*, 69: 57–81.

Cmnd 4014 (1998) *Modern Local Government: In Touch with the People*, London: The Stationary Office.

Coates, D. (2000) 'New Labour's Industrial and Employment Policy', in D. Coates and P. Lawler (eds) *New Labour in Power*, Manchester: Manchester University Press, pp. 122–35.

Coats, D. (2004) *Speaking Up! Voice, Industrial Democracy and Organisational Performance*, London: Work Foundation.

Coats, D. (2007) 'Hard Labour: The Future of Work and the Role of Public Policy', in G. Hassan (ed.) *After Blair: Politics after the New Labour Decade*, London: Lawrence and Wishart, pp. 131–45.

Cohen, J. and Rogers, J. (1995) 'Secondary Associations and Democratic Governance', in J. Cohen and J. Rogers (eds) *Associations and Democracy*, London: Verso, pp. 7–100.

Confederation of British Industry (CBI) (2003) *High Performance Workplaces: The Role of Employee Involvement in a Modern Economy – CBI Response*, London: CBI.

Cooper, C., Dewe, P. and O'Driscoll, M. (2001) *Organizational Stress: A Review and Critique of Theory, Research and Applications*, London: Sage.

Cressey, P. and Scott, P. (1992) 'Employment Technology and Industrial Relations in Clearing Banks – Is the Honeymoon Over?', *New Technology, Work and Employment*, 7: 2, 83–94.

Crouch, C. (1992) 'The Fate of Articulated Industrial Relations Systems: A Stock-Taking after the Neo-Liberal Decade', in M. Regini (ed.) *The Future of Labour Movements*, London: Sage.

Croucher, R. (1982) *Engineers at War: 1939–1945*, London: Merlin.

Cully, M., Woodland, S., O'Reilly, A. and Dix, G. (1999) *Britain at Work*, London: Routledge.

Danford, A. (1999) *Japanese Management Techniques and British Workers*, London: Routledge.

Danford, A., Richardson, M. and Upchurch, M. (2003) *New Unions, New Workplaces: A Study of Union Resilience in the Restructured Workplace*, London: Routledge.

Danford, A., Richardson, M., Stewart, P., Tailby, S. and Upchurch, M. (2005) *Partnership and the High Performance Workplace: Work and Employment Relations in the Aerospace Industry*, Basingstoke: Palgrave Macmillan.

Danford, A., Richardson, M., Stewart, P., Tailby, S. and Upchurch, M. (2007) 'Capital Mobility, Job Loss and Union Strategy: The Case of the UK Aerospace Industry', *Labor Studies Journal*, 32(3): 298–318.

Darlington, R. (1994) *The Dynamics of Workplace Unionism: Shop Stewards' Organization in Three Merseyside Plants*, London: Continuum.

Delbridge, R. (1998) *Life on the Line in Contemporary Manufacturing*, Oxford: Oxford University Press.

Department of Health (1998) *Working Together – Securing a Quality Workforce for the NHS*, London: Department of Health.

Department of Health (1999) *Report of the NHS Taskforce on Staff Involvement*, London: Department of Health.

Department of Health (2000) *The NHS Plan: A Plan for Investment, a Plan for Reform*, London: Department of Health.

Department of Health (2002) *HR in the NHS Plan*, London: Department of Health.

Department of Health (2003) *Staff Involvement: Better Decisions, Better Care*, London: Department of Health.

Department of Health (2005) *A Short Guide to NHS Foundation Trusts*, www.dh.gov.uk/en/Publicationsandstatistics.

Department of Health (2007) *Partnership Agreement: An Agreement between DH, NHS Employers and NHS Trade Unions*, London: Department of Health.

Department of Trade and Industry (DTI) (1998) *Fairness at Work*, Cmnd 3968, London: HMSO.

Department for Trade and Industry (2002) *High Performance Workplaces: The Role of Employee Involvement in a Modern Economy*, London: DTI.

Department of Trade and Industry (2004) *Achieving Best Practice in Your Business. Maximising Potential: High Performance Workplaces,* London: DTI.

Docherty, P., Forslin, J. and Shani, A. B. (2002) 'Sustainable Work Systems' in P. Docherty, J. Forslin and A. B. Shani (eds) *Creating Sustainable Work Systems,* London: Routledge, pp. 213–25.

Driffield, N. (1999) 'Indirect Employment Effects of Foreign Direct Investment into the UK', *Bulletin of Economic Research,* 51(3): 207–21.

Dundon, T. and Rollinson, D. (2004) *Employment Relations in Non-Union Firms,* London: Routledge.

Dunne, P. and Macdonald, G. (2001) 'Procurement in the Post Cold War World: A Case Study of the UK', in C. Sefati, M. Brzoska, B. Hagelin, I. Goudie, E. Skons, W. Smit and R. Weidacher (eds) *The Restructuring of the European Defence Industry: Dynamics of Change,* European Commission, Directorate-General for Research, COST Action A10.

EEF (2001) *Catching Up with Uncle Sam: The Final Report on US/UK Manufacturing Productivity,* London: Engineering Employers Federation.

EEF/CIPD (2003) *Maximising Employee Potential and Business Performance: The Role of High Performance Working,* London: CIPD.

Elger, T. and Smith, C. (2005) *Assembling Work: Remaking Factory Regimes in Japanese Multinationals in Britain,* Oxford: OUP.

Fairbrother, P. (1996) 'Workplace Trade Unionism in the State Sector', in P. Ackers, C. Smith and P. Smith (eds) *The New Workplace and Trade Unionism,* London: Routledge, pp. 110–48.

Fairbrother, P. (2000) *Trade Unions at the Crossroads,* London: Mansell.

Findlay, P. and McKinlay, A. (2003) 'Organising in Electronics: Recruitment, Recognition and Retention – Shadow Shop Stewards in Scotland's "Silicon Glen"', in G. Gall (ed.) *Union Organising, Campaigning for Union Recognition,* London: Routledge.

Forth, J. and Millward, N. (2002) *The Growth of Direct Communication,* London: CIPD.

Fox, A. (1974) *Beyond Contract: Work, Power and Trust Relations,* London: Faber and Faber.

Freeman, R. and Medoff, J. (1984) *What Do Unions Do?* New York: Basic Books.

Gall, G. (1999) 'Union Resilience in a Cold Climate: The Case of the UK Banking Industry', in M. Upchurch (ed.) *The State and Globalisation: Comparative Studies of Labour and Capital in National Economies,* London: Mansell, pp. 113–42.

Gall, G. (2001a) 'From Adversarialism to Partnership? Trade Unionism and Industrial Relations in the Banking Sector in the UK', *Employee Relations,* 23(4): 353–75.

Gall, G. (2001b) 'Management Control Approaches and Union Recognition in Britain', *Paper presented to the Work, Employment and Society Conference,* Nottingham, September.

Gall, G. (2004) 'Trade Union Recognition in Britain, 1995–2002: Turning a Corner?', *Industrial Relations Journal,* 35(3): 250–70.

Gall, G. (2005) 'Breaking with, and Breaking, "Partnership": The Case of the Postal Workers and Royal Mail in Britain', in M. Stuart and M. Martínez Lucio (eds) *Partnership and Modernisation in Employment Relations*, London, Routledge, pp. 154–70.

Gallie, D., Felstead, A. and Green, F. (2001) 'Employer Policies and Organizational Commitment in Britain, 1992–1997', *Journal of Management Studies*, 38(8): 1081–101.

Gallie, D., Felstead, A. and Green, F. (2004) 'Changing Patterns of Task Discretion in Britain', *Work, Employment and Society*, 18(2): 243–66.

Gallie, D., White, M., Cheng, Y. and Tomlinson, M. (1998) *Restructuring the Employment Relationship*, Oxford: Oxford University Press.

Geary, J. F. and Roche, W. K. (2003) 'Workplace Partnership and the Displaced Activist Thesis', *Industrial Relations Journal*, 34(1): 32–51.

Geddes, M. (2001) 'What About the Workers? Best Value, Employment and Work in Local Public Services' *Policy & Politics*, 29(4): 497–508.

Geddes, M. and Martin, S. (2000) 'The Policy and Politics of Best Value: Currents, Crosscurrents and Undercurrents in the New Regime', *Policy & Politics*, 8(3): 379–95.

Giddens, A. (1990) 'Socialism, Modernity and Utopianism', in *New Statesman and Society*, 2 November, pp. 20–2, reprinted (1992), in S. Hall, D. Held and A. McGrew (eds) *Modernity and Its Futures*, Cambridge: Open University/Polity.

Giddens, A. (1998) *The Third Way*, Cambridge: Polity.

Giddens, A. (2000) *The Third Way and Its Critics*, Cambridge: Polity.

Givan, R. and Bach, S. (2007) 'Workforce Responses to the Creeping Privatization of the UK National Health Service', *International Labor and Working-Class History*, 71: 133–53.

Godard, J. (2001) 'Beyond the High-Performance Paradigm? An Analysis of Variation in Canadian Managerial Perceptions of Reform Programme Effectiveness', *British Journal of Industrial Relations*, 39(1): 25–52.

Godard, J. (2004) 'A Critical Assessment of the High-Performance Paradigm', *British Journal of Industrial Relations*, 42(2): 349–78.

Gollan, P. (2000) 'Non-Union Forms of Employee Representation in the United Kingdom and Australia', in B. E. Kaufman and D. G. Taras (eds) *Non-Union Employee Representation: History, Contemporary Practice, and Policy*, New York: M. E. Sharpe, pp. 410–49.

Gollan, P. (2005) 'Silent Voices: Representation at the Eurotunnel Call Centre', *Employee Relations*, 34(4): 423–50.

Gospel, H. and Willman, P. (2003) 'Dilemmas in Worker Representation', in H. Gospel and S. Wood (eds) *Representing Workers*, London: Routledge, pp. 144–65.

Gramsci, A. (1971) *Selections from the Prison Notebooks*, London: Lawrence and Wishart.

Green, F. (2001) 'It's Been a Hard Day's Night: The Concentration and Intensification of Work in Late Twentieth Century Britain', *British Journal of Industrial Relations*, 39(1): 53–80.

Green, F. (2006) *Demanding Work: The Paradox of Job Quality in the Affluent Economy*, Princeton, NJ: Princeton University Press.

Green, R., Steen, M. and Wilson, A. (2001) 'The Third Way in Europe: New Labour's Employment and Industrial Relations Strategy', in D. Foden,

J. Hoffman and R. Scott (eds) *Globalisation and the Social Contract*, Brussels, European Trade Union Institute, pp. 97–114.

Greene, A., Black, J. and Ackers, P. (2000) 'The Union Makes Us Strong? A Study of the Dynamics of Workplace Union Leadership at Two UK Manufacturing Plants', *British Journal of Industrial Relations*, 38(1): 75–93.

Guest, D. and Conway, N. (2004) 'Exploring the Paradox of Unionised Worker Dissatisfaction', *Industrial Relations Journal*, 35(2): 102–21.

Guest, D. and Hoque, K. (1994) 'The Good, the Bad, and the Ugly: Employment Relations in New Non-Union Workplaces', *Human Resource Management Journal*, 5(1): 1–14.

Guest, D., Michie, J., Conway, N. and Sheehan, M. (2003) 'Human Resource Management and Corporate Performance in the UK', *British Journal of Industrial Relations*, 41(2): 219–314.

Guest, D. and Peccei, R. (2001) 'Partnership at Work: Mutuality and the Balance of Advantage', *British Journal of Industrial Relations*, 39(2): 207–36.

Hall, M. and Terry, M. (2004) 'The Emerging System of Statutory Worker Representation', in G. Healy, E. Heery, P. Taylor and W. Brown (eds) *The Future of Worker Representation*, Basingstoke: Palgrave Macmillan.

Hayes, B. (2006) *Billy Hayes Blog*, http://www.billyhayes.co.uk/permalink.php?id=P640010C (accessed 1 March 2007).

Haynes, P. and Allen, M. (2001) 'Partnership as Union Strategy: A preliminary evaluation', *Employee Relations*, 23(2): 164–87.

Head, S. (2003) *The New Ruthless Economy: Work and Power in the Digital Age*, NY: Oxford University Press.

Heckscher, C. (1996) *The New Unionism: Employee Involvement in the Changing Corporation*, Ithaca, NY: ILR Press.

Heery, E. (2002) 'Partnership versus Organising: Alternative Futures for British Trade Unionism', *Industrial Relations Journal*, 33(1): 21–35.

Heery, E., Conley, H., Delbridge, R. and Stewart, P. (2005) 'Seeking Partnership for the Contingent Workforce', in M. Stuart and M. Martínez Lucio (eds) *Partnership and Modernisation in Employment Relations*, London: Routledge, pp. 171–87.

Hirschman, A. O. (1970) *Exit, Voice and Loyalty: Responses to Decline in Firms, Organisations and States*, Cambridge, MA: Harvard University Press.

Hirst, P. (1994) *Associative Democracy: New Forms of Economic and Social Governance*, London: Polity.

Hirst, P. (1997) *From Statism to Pluralism*, London: UCL Press.

HMSO (1998) 'Fairness at Work' White Paper: Employment Relations Bill, Cm3863, London: HMSO.

House of Commons Trade and Industry Committee (2005) *The UK Aerospace Industry: Fifteenth Report of Session 2004–5*, London: The Stationery Office.

Huselid, M. A. (1995) 'The Impact of Human Resource Management Practices on Turnover, Productivity and Corporate Financial Performance', *Academy of Management Journal*, 38: 655–72.

Hyman, R. (1975) *Industrial Relations: A Marxist Introduction*, Basingstoke: Macmillan.

Hyman, R. (2005) 'Whose (Social) Partnership?', in M. Stuart and M. Martínez Lucio (eds) *Partnership and Modernisation in Employment Relations*, London: Routledge, pp. 251–65.

Involvement and Participation Association (1997) *Towards Industrial Partnership*, London: IPA.

Jenkins, J. (2007) 'Gambling Partners? The Risky Outcomes of Workplace Partnerships', *Work, Employment and Society*, 21: 635–52.

Johnstone, S., Ackers, P. and Wilkinson, A. (2005) 'The Process and Practice of Partnership: Case Studies from the UK Financial Services Sector', *Paper presented to the British Universities Industrial Relations Association Conference*, University of Northumbria, Newcastle, July.

Katz, R. and Allen, T. J. (1985) 'Project Performance and the Locus of Influence in the R&D Matrix', *Academy of Management Journal*, 1: 67–87.

Kelly, G., Kelly, D. and Gamble, A. (1997) 'Conclusion: Stakeholder Capitalism', in G. Kelly, D. Kelly and A. Gamble (eds) *Stakeholder Capitalism*, London: Macmillan, pp. 238–56.

Kelly, G. and Parkinson, J. (2001) 'The Conceptual Foundations of the Company: A Pluralist Approach', in J. Parkinson, A. Gamble and G. Kelly (eds) *The Political Economy of the Company*, London: Hart Publishing.

Kelly, J. (1996) 'Union Militancy and Social Partnership', in P. Ackers, C. Smith and P. Smith (eds) *The New Workplace and Trade Unionism*, London: Routledge, pp. 77–109.

Kelly, J. (2004) 'Social Partnership Agreements in Britain: Labor Cooperation and Compliance', *Industrial Relations*, 43(1): 267–92.

Kelly, J. (2005) 'Social Partnership Agreements in Britain', in M. Stuart and M. Martínez Lucio (eds) *Partnership and Modernisation in Employment Relations*, London, Routledge, pp. 188–209.

Kersley, B., Alpin, C., Forth, J., Bryson, A., Bewley, H., Dix, G. and Oxenbridge, S. (2006) *Inside the Workplace: Findings from the 2004 Workplace Employment Relations Survey*, London: Routledge.

Kessler, I. and Heron, P. (2001) 'Steward Organization in a Professional Union: The Case of the Royal College of Nursing', *British Journal of Industrial Relations*, 39(3): 367–92.

Kim, Dong-One and Kim, Hyun-Ki (2004) 'A Comparison of the Effectiveness of Unions and Non-Union Works Councils in Korea: Can Non-Union Employee Representation Substitute for Trade Unionism?', *International Journal of Human Resource Management*, 15(6): 1069–93.

Kinnie, N., Hutchinson, S., Purcell, J., Rayton, B. and Swart, J. (2005) 'Satisfaction with HR Practices and Commitment to the Organisation: Why One Size Does Not Fit All', *Human Resource Management Journal*, 15(4): 9–29.

Kochan, T., Katz, H. and McKersie, R. (1986) *The Transformation of American Industrial Relations*, New York: Basic Books.

Kochan, T. and Osterman, P. (1994) *The Mutual Gains Enterprise*, Boston, Massachusetts: Harvard University Press.

Kristensen, J. E. (2001) 'Corporate Social Responsibility and New Social Partnerships', in C. Kjægaard and S-Å Westphalen (eds) *From Collective*

Bargaining to Social Partnerships: New Roles of the Social Partners in Europe, Copenhagen, The Copenhagen Centre, pp. 21–37.

Labour Force Survey (2006) London: Office of National Statistics.

Lincoln, J. and Kalleberg, A. (1990) *Culture, Control and Commitment: A Study of Work, Work Organization and Work Attitudes in the United States and Japan*, Cambridge: Cambridge University Press.

Lloyd, C. (2001) 'What Do Employee Councils Do? The Impact of Non-Union Forms of Representation on Trade Union Organisation', *Industrial Relations Journal*, 32(4): 313–27.

Lloyd, C. and Payne, J. (2006) 'Goodbye to All That? A Critical Re-Evaluation of the Role of High Performance Work Organization within the UK Skills Debate', *Work, Employment and Society*, 20(1): 151–65.

Makin, P., Cooper, C. and Cox, C. (1996) *Organisations and the Psychological Contract: Managing People at Work*, The British Psychological Society.

Marchington, M. (1994) 'The Dynamics of Joint Consultation', in K. Sisson (ed.) *Personnel Management*, Oxford: Blackwell, pp. 662–93.

Marchington, M. and Wilkinson, A. (2000) 'Direct Participation', in S. Bach and K. Sisson (eds) *Personnel Management* (Third edition), Oxford: Blackwell, pp. 340–64.

Marks, A., Findlay, T., Hine, J., McKinlay, A. and Thompson, P. (1998) 'The Politics of Partnership? Innovation in Employment Relations in the Scottish Spirits Industry', *British Journal of Industrial Relations*, 36(2): 209–26.

Martin, S. (2000) 'Implementing "Best Value": Local Public Services in Transition', *Public Administration*, 78(1): 209–27.

Martin, S., Davis, H., Bovaird, A., Downe, J., Geddes, M., Hartley, J., Lewis, M., Sanderson, I. and Sapwell, P. (2001) *Improving Local Public Services: Final Evaluation of the Best Value Pilot Programme*, London: HMSO, p. 152.

Martínez Lucio, M. and Stuart, M. (2000) 'Swimming against the Tide: Social Partnership, Mutual Gains and the Revival of "Tired" HRM', *Working Paper 00/03*, The Centre for Industrial Relations and Human Resource Management, Leeds University, Leeds.

Martínez Lucio, M. and Stuart, M. (2002) 'Assessing Partnership: The Prospects for, and Challenges of, Modernisation', *Employee Relations*, 23(3): 252–61.

Martínez Lucio, M. and Stuart, M. (2005) '"Partnership" and New Industrial Relations in a Risk Society: An Age of Shotgun Weddings and Marriages of Convenience', *Work, Employment and Society*, 19(4): 797–817.

McIlroy, J. (1995) *Trade Unions in Britain Today*, Manchester : Manchester University Press.

McIlroy, J. (1998) 'The Enduring Alliance? Trade Unions and the Making of New Labour 1994–97', *British Journal of Industrial Relations*, 36(4): 537–64.

McIlroy, J. (2000) 'New Labour, New Unions, New Left', in *Capital & Class*, (71): 11–47.

McLoughlin, I. and Gourlay, S. (1994) *Enterprise without Unions: Industrial Relations in the Non-Union Firm*, Buckingham: Open University Press.

Mehri, D. (2005) *Notes from Toyota Land: An American Engineer in Japan*, Ithaca and London: ILR Press.

Metcalf, D. (2005) 'Trade Unions: Resurgence or Perdition? An Economic Analysis', in S. Fernie and D. Metcalf (eds) *Trade Unions: Resurgence or Demise?*, London: Routledge.

Michie, J. and Sheehan, M. (2003) 'Labour Flexibility – Securing Management's Right to Manage Badly?', in B. Burchell, S. Deakin, J. Michie and J. Rubery (eds) *Systems of Production, Markets, Organisations and Performance*, London: Routledge.

Monks, J. (2000) *Address to the Institute of Directors Convention by TUC General Secretary John Monks*, Press Release, TUC, London, 19 April.

Monks, J. (2006) Quoted in 'Rise of "casino capitalism" Shakes Faith of Moderate Monks' by Stefan Stern in *Financial Times*, 20 November.

Moran, M. (1991) *The Politics of the Financial Services Revolution*, London: Macmillan.

Morris, M., Storey, J., Wilkinson, A. and Cressey, P. (2001) 'Industry Change and Union Mergers in British Retail Finance', *British Journal of Industrial Relations*, 39(2): 237–56.

Murman, E., Allen, T., Bozdogan, K., Cutcher-Gershenfeld, J., McManus, H., Nightingale, D., Rebentisch, E., Shields, T., Stahl, F., Walton, M., Warmkessel, J., Weiss, S. and Widnall, S. (2002) *Lean Enterprise Value: Insights from MIT's Lean Aerospace Initiative*, Basingstoke: Palgrave Macmillan.

Nelson, N. and Wright, S. (1994) *Power and Participation*, London: Intermediate Technology Publications.

Nichols, T. and Cam, S. (2005) *Labour in a Global World – The Case of White Goods*, Basingstoke: Palgrave Macmillan.

Novitz, T. (2002) 'A Revised Role for Trade Unions as Designed by New Labour: The Representation Pyramid and "Partnership"', *Journal of Law and Society*, 29(3): 487–509.

Office of Public Services Reform (2002) *Reforming Our Public Services*, The Prime Minister's Office of Public Services Reform.

Oxenbridge, S. and Brown, W. (2002) 'The Two Faces of Partnership? An Assessment of Partnership and Co-Operative Employer/Trade Union Relationships', *Employee Relations*, 24(3): 262–76.

Oxenbridge, S. and Brown, W. (2004a) 'Achieving a New Equilibrium? The Stability of Co-Operative Employer–Union Relationships', *Industrial Relations Journal*, 35(5): 388–402.

Oxenbridge, S. and Brown, W. (2004b) 'A Poisoned Chalice? Trade Union Representatives in Partnership and Co-Operative Employer–Union Relationships', in G. Healy, E. Heery, P. Taylor and W. Brown (eds) *The Future of Worker Representation*, Basingstoke: Palgrave Macmillan/ESRC, pp. 187–206.

Personnel Today (2005) *Partnership Working*, http://www.personneltoday.com/Articles/2005/12/06/32899/partnership-working.html (accessed 27 February 2007).

Pollock, Alison (2007) 'What Sicko Doesn't Tell You ...', *The Guardian*, 24 September.

Porter, M. (2003) *UK Competitiveness: Moving to the Next Stage*, London: Department of Trade and Industry (2003).

Porter, M. and Ketels (2003) 'UK Competitiveness: Moving to the Next Stage', *DTI Economics Paper No. 3*, London: DTI.

Prabhakar, R. (2003) *Stakeholding and New Labour*, Basingstoke: Palgrave Macmillan.

Radcliffe, T. (1997) 'The Changing Face of Employee Representative Organisation in the Retail Banking and Building Society Sector', *MSc Dissertation*, UMIST.

Ramsay, H. (1977) 'Cycles of Control', *Sociology*, 11(3): 481–506.

Ramsay, H. (1996) 'Involvement, Empowerment and Commitment', in B. Towers (ed.) *The Handbook of Human Resource Management*, Oxford: Blackwell.

Richardson, M., Danford, A., Tailby, S., Stewart, P. and Upchurch, M. (2005) 'Best Value and Workplace Partnership in Local Government', *Personnel Review* (Special Issue on Employment Relations and Public Services – 'Modernisation' under Labour), 34(6): 713–28.

Rinehart, J., Huxley, C. and Robertson, D. (1997) *Just Another Car Factory? Lean Production and Its Discontents*, Ithaca and London: ILR Press.

Roper, I., Higgins, P. and James, P. (2007) 'Shaping the Bargaining Agenda: The Audit Commission and Public Service Reform in the British Local Government', *International Journal of Human Resource Management*, 18(9): 1589–1607.

Rose, M. (2003) 'Good Deal, Bad Deal? Job Satisfaction in Occupations', *Work, Employment and Society*, 17(3): 503–30.

Rothschild, J. (2000) 'Creating a Just and Democratic Workplace: More Engagement, Less Hierarchy', *Contemporary Sociology*, 29(1): 195–213.

Roy, D. (1980) 'Repression and Incorporation. Fear Stuff, Sweet Stuff and Evil Stuff: Management's Defenses against Unionization in the South', in T. Nichols (ed.) *Capital and Labour: A Marxist Primer*, Glasgow: Fontana.

Rubery, J. (1988) *Employers and the Labour Market*, Oxford: Blackwell.

Rubery, J. (1994) 'The British Production Regime: A Societal-Specific System?', *Economy and Society*, 23(3): 335–54.

Rubery, J., Grimshaw, D., Donnelly, R. and Urwin, P. (2005) 'Revisiting the UK Model: From Basket Case to Success Story?', *EWERC Paper*, Manchester University Business School, UK.

Samuel, P. (2005) 'Partnership Working and the Cultivated Activist', *Industrial Relations Journal*, 36(1): 59–76.

Samuel, P. (2007) 'Partnership Consultation and Employer Domination in Two British Life and Pensions Firms', *Work, Employment and Society*, 21(3): 459–78.

SBAC (2000) *The Competitiveness Challenge: People Management in Aerospace*, London: The Society of British Aerospace Companies.

SBAC (2003) *UK Aerospace Facts and Figures*, London: The Society of British Aerospace Companies.

SBAC (2007) *UK Aerospace Industry Survey*, London: The Society of British Aerospace Companies.

Sennett, R. *The Corrosion of Character: The Unexpected Decline of Leisure*, New York: Basic Books.

Shifrin, Tash (2004) 'Government Reveals NHS Price List', *The Guardian*, 6 February.

Sisson, K. (1995) 'Change and Continuity in British Industrial Relations', in R. Locke, T. Kochan, and M. Piore (eds) *Employment Relations in a Changing World Economy*, Cambridge, MA: MIT Press.

Smith, C. (1987) *Technical Workers: Class, Labour and Trade Unionism*, Basingstoke: Macmillan.

Snape, E., Redman, T. and Wilkinson, A. (1993) 'Human Resource Management in Building Societies: Making the Transformation', *Human Resource Management Journal*, 2(4): 43–60.

Soskice, D. (1996) 'Stakeholding Yes; the German Model No' in *Prospect* (April, Issue 7).

Stewart, P., Lewchuk, W., Yates, C., Saruta, M. and Danford, A. (2004) 'Patterns of Labour Control and the Erosion of Labour Standards: Towards an International Study of the Quality of Working Life in the Automobile Industry (Canada, Japan and the UK)', in E. Charron and P. Stewart (eds) *Work and Employment Relations in the Automobile Industry*, Basingstoke: Palgrave Macmillan.

Stewart, P. and Wass, V. (1998) 'From "embrace and change" to "engage and change": Trade Union Renewal and the New Management Strategies in the UK Automotive Industry', *New Technology, Work and Employment*, 13(2): 77–93.

Storey, J., Wilkinson, A., Cressey, P. and Morris, T. (1998) 'Employment Relations in UK Banking', in M. Regini, J. Kitay and M. Beatheoge (eds) *Changing Employment Relations in Banking*, MIT Press, Cambridge, MA.

Stuart, M. and Martínez Lucio, M. (2000) 'Renewing the Model Employer', *Journal of Management in Medicine*, 14(5–6): 310–26.

Stuart, M. and Martínez Lucio, M. (2005) 'Partnership and Modernisation in Employment Relations: An Introduction', in Stuart, M. and Martínez Lucio, M. (eds) *Partnership and Modernisation in Employment Relations*, London: Routledge.

Tailby, S., Richardson, M., Stewart, P., Danford, A. and Upchurch, M. (2004) 'Partnership at Work and Worker Participation: An NHS Case Study', *Industrial Relations Journal*, 35(5): 403–18.

Tailby, S., Richardson, M., Upchurch, M., Danford, A. and Stewart, P. (2007) 'Partnership with and without Trade Unions in the UK Financial Services: Filling or Fuelling the Representation Gap?', *Industrial Relations Journal*, 38(3): 210–28.

Taylor, P. and Ramsay, H. (1998) 'Unions, Partnership and HRM: Sleeping with the Enemy?', *International Journal of Employment Studies*, 6(2): 115–43.

Taylor, R. (2004) *Partnership at Work: The Way to Corporate Renewal?*, Swindon: ESRC.

Terry, M. (1995) 'Trade Unions: Shop Stewards and the Workplace', in P. Edwards (ed.) *Industrial Relations: Theory and Practice*, Oxford: Blackwell.

Terry, M. (1999) 'Systems of Collective Employee Representation in Non-Union Firms in the UK', *Industrial Relations Journal*, 30(1): 16–30.

Terry, M. (2003) 'Can "Partnership" Reverse the Decline of British Trade Unions?', *Work, Employment and Society*, 17(3): 459–72.

Terry, M. and Smith, J. (2003) 'Evaluation of the Partnership at Work Fund', *Employment Relations Research Series No. 17*, London: Department of Trade and Industry.

Thompson, N. (1996) 'Supply Side Socialism: The Political Economy of New Labour', *New Left Review*, 216.

Trades Union Congress (1999) *Partners for Progress: New Unionism at the Workplace*, London: TUC.

Trades Union Congress (2000) 'Partnership Adds Value for Unions and Employers in the South West', www.tuc.org.uk/partnership/tuc-763-f0.cfm.

Trades Union Congress (2001) *Partnership in Depth*, TUC Partnership Institute, www.tuc.org.uk/pi/partnership.ht.

Trades Union Congress (2002) *Partnership, Performance and Employment: A Review of the Evidence*, TUC Partnership Institute, www.tuc.org.uk/pi/research.htm.

Trades Union Congress (2003) *Congress Report of Decisions*, http://www.tuc.org.uk/congress/tuc-7138-f0.cfm (accessed 1 March 2007).

Trade Union Congress (2006) 'Focus on Health and Safety: Trade Union Trends Survey', *TUC Biennial Survey of Safety Representatives*, London: 2006.

Trades Union Congress/EO (1999) *The Time of Our Lives in Bristol*, London: TUC/Employers Organisation for Local Government.

TUC Partnership Institute (2000) *Partners for Progress, Winning at Work*, London: Trades Union Congress.

TUC/CBI (2001) *The UK Productivity Challenge*, CBI/TUC Submission to the Productivity Initiative.

UNISON (2002) *Best Value and the Two-Tier Workforce in Local Government*, Best Value Intelligence Unit, London: UNISON.

Upchurch, M. and Danford, A. (2001) 'Industrial Restructuring, "Globalisation", and the Trade Union Response: A Study of MSF in the South West of England', *New Technology, Work and Employment*, 16(2): 100–14.

Upchurch, M., Tailby, S., Richardson, M., Danford, A. and Stewart, P. (2006) 'Employee Representation and Partnership in the Non-Union Sector: A Paradox of Intention?', *Human Resource Management Journal*, 16(4): 393–410.

Waddington, J. (2001) 'United Kingdom: Restructuring Services Within a De-regulated Regime', in D. E. Dolvik (ed.) *At Your Service? Comparative Perspectives on Employment and Labour Relations in the European Private Sector Services*, SALTSA, Work and Society, 27.

White, M., Hill, S., McGovern, P., Mills, C. and Smeaton, D. (2003) '"High-performance" Management Practices, Working Hours and Work-Life Balance', *British Journal of Industrial Relations*, 41(2): 175–95.

White, M., Hill, S., Mills, C. and Smeaton, D. (2004) *Managing to Change? British Workplaces and the Future of Work*. Basingstoke: Palgrave Macmillan.

Whitfield, D. (2001) *Public Services or Corporate Welfare: Rethinking the Nation State in the Global Economy*, Pluto.

Williamson, J. (1997) 'Your Stake at Work: The TUC's Agenda', in G. Kelly, D. Kelly and A. Gamble (eds) *Stakeholder Capitalism*, London: Macmillan, pp. 155–68.

Willman, P., Bryson, A. and Gomez, R. (2003) 'Why Do Voice Regimes Differ?' *Centre for Economic Performance Working Paper*, London School of Economics.

Wills, J. (2000) 'Great Expectations: Three Years in the Life of a European Works Council', *European Journal of Industrial Relations*, 6(1): 85–107.

Wills, J. (2004) 'Trade Unionism and Partnership in Practice: Evidence from the Barclays-UNIFI Agreement', *Industrial Relations Journal*, 35(4): 329–43.

Winchester, D. (2005) 'Agreement on Implementation of Pay Reforms in National Health Service', *EIROnline*, 28 January.

Index

ACAS 13
ACTSS 136
adversarialism 14, 23, 55–6, 83, 167
AEEU 158, 161
agency staff 39, 98, 134, 167
Agenda for Change (in the NHS)
    109–10
Airbus 133
Alliance for Finance 56
al-Qaeda 158
Amicus 16, 18, 56, 129, 136, 154–8
APEX 136
ASTMS 55
Audit Commission 104

BAe Systems 133
Bank, Insurance and Finance Union
    (BIFU) 56–8
Barclays Bank 58
Blair, Tony 4, 6, 168
Blue Circle 16
Borg Warner 171
British Aerospace 134
Brown, Gordon 6, 13
business unionism 5, 9

Cabinet Office 5
CBI (Confederation of British
    Industry) 7
Certification Office 56
China 133
CIPD 7, 173
closed shop 68
collective bargaining 26, 148, 171
communications
    email 103
    top down/downward 105, 116,
        118–20
    two-way 71
compulsory competitive tendering
    84–7, 94

computer technology 97, 103
    see also information technology
Conservative (governments) 84,
    107, 108
corporate governance 62, 166
    see also, shareholder, stakeholder
corporate social responsibility 12
Co-Operative bank 59
customer focus 96
CWU (Communication Workers'
    Union) 18

democracy
    associative 13
    industrial 11
    participative 13
    representative 13–14
Department of Health 107–8, 116,
    124, 129–30
Department of Trade and Industry
    7, 18
Direct Line 53

EEF (Engineering Employers'
    Federation) 7
employee commitment 37–40, 51
employee involvement 82
    in Best Value 85, 90, 101–3
    in NHS Trust 122
employee voice 11, 54, 60, 109,
    117, 150
ethics and ethical socialism 14
ETUC (European Trade Union
    Confederation) 173
European Union
    Charter of Fundamental Rights
        8
    European Works Council (and
        Directive) 5, 57, 151, 153
    Lisbon Summit 6
    Social Model 11–12

Fairness at Work   4, 86
flexibility   30, 63, 119, 141, 146
   functional   30
   new flexible firm   134
   numerical   134
   skills   69

gender   23, 46
   see also women workers
General Strike (1926)   11
Germany, German   63, 137
GMB   87
good employer   109
   see also model employer
Guild of Insurance Officers   55

Hayes, Billy   18
high performance working   2, 7,
   14, 20–5, 134, 174
human resource management   15,
   58, 61, 109

ideology (of partnership)   4–5, 12,
   84, 167, 174
industrial democracy   11
Information and Consultation of
   Employees Regulations   5, 57,
   60, 137, 153, 160
information technology (ICT)   20, 53
   see also computer technology
Inland Revenue   16
Involvement and Participation
   Association (IPA)   5
Italy, Italian   137

John Lewis   65
job evaluation   72
job insecurity/security   9, 21, 93,
   132, 144, 150, 158, 166
job rotation   63
job satisfaction   34–6, 90, 166
   in local government authority
      98–100

kaizen   21, 142–3
knowledge work(ers)   48, 54

lean production   22
Legal and General   16
Low Pay Commission   13

Manpower (Staff Agency)   16
marketisation   107–8
model employer   39
   see also good employer
Mond-Turner Agreement   11
Monks, John   9, 173
MSF (Manufacturing, Science and
   Finance Union)   113, 136, 148,
   156
mutuality, mutual interest, mutual
   gain   3, 22, 82, 163

National Union of Bank
   Employees   55
neoliberalism   15, 21, 51–2, 134,
   167
neo-pluralism   106, 165
neo-unitarism   2
New Labour (government)   5, 6, 13,
   17, 147, 168, 172
   and Best Value   85–6
   and neoliberalism   15, 134
new realism   4
New Right   133
New York   158
non-union(ism)   40, 59–61, 102
nurses   120–2

outsourcing   143

Partnership at Work Fund   2
paternalism   53–4, 57
PCS (Public and Commercial
   Services Union)   18
performance related pay   54, 63,
   72
pluralist, pluralism   2, 11, 14
Private Finance Initiative   108
productivity
   coalition   165, 169
   labour productivity   21–2
   UK productivity gap   5–6

professional associations, unions 110, 127
post-Fordism 34

quality circles 23–4
quality of working life 22, 27, 34, 44, 106, 167

R&D (research and development) 138
Rhenish Model (of capitalism) 174
Rolls Royce 134
Royal College of Nursing (RCN) 112, 127
Royal Mail 16

Scottish Power 16
shareholders 10, 52
single union deals 4
skills, training 20, 25, 30, 41, 54, 69
social capital 12, 14
social cohesion 105, 168, 175
staff associations 54, 56
 AXA 58
 Britannia Building Society 58
 NatWest 58
stakeholders, stakeholderism 10, 89
stress at work 22, 44–7, 145, 162
strikes 149, 166
suggestion schemes 76
surveillance 139
sustainable work system 12

task discretion 27, 30–2, 166
team briefing 25, 116
team-working and teams 7, 23, 63, 145
temporary staff 98, 134

TGWU (Transport and General Workers' Union) 87–90, 96, 136, 149
Third Way 159, 174
 and partnership 10–12
trade unions
 craft 133
 effectiveness of 50, 78, 92, 168
 finance sector 56–8
 full-time officials 2, 16, 89
 and high performance working 47–8
 lay officials 90, 112
 and partnership 111, 115, 130
 rank-and-file members 15–16, 18, 48, 172
trust (between employer and employee) 9, 55, 141, 152, 156, 169, 173
TUC
 and partnership 7–9, 17, 170
 Partnership Institute 9, 171

UCATT 87
UNiFI 56, 58
UNIFI 56
UNISON 87–8, 112
UNITE 18, 56, 68, 136
Union Learning Representatives 5
Union of Insurance Staffs 55
United Distillers 16
USA 132, 134, 137–8
utopian realism 174

Wales, Welsh 63, 68
women workers 46
 see also gender
Work Foundation 174
work intensification 27–9, 98, 102, 118, 169
work-life balance 119